PHILIP R. SCHATZ
Attorney At Law
36 West 44th St. Suite 1111
New York, NY 10036
(212) 840-2980

9/25
STRAND PRICE
$5.00

"Making Sure We Are True to Our Founders"

"MAKING SURE WE ARE TRUE TO OUR FOUNDERS"

The Association of the Bar of the City of New York, 1970–95

JEFFREY B. MORRIS

ILLUSTRATED
WITH PHOTOGRAPHS

FORDHAM UNIVERSITY PRESS
New York
1997

Library of Congress Cataloging-in-Publication Data

Morris, Jeffrey Brandon, 1941–
    Making sure we are true to our founders : The Association of the
Bar of the City of New York, 1970–95 / Jeffrey B. Morris ;
illustrated with photographs.
        p.   cm.
    Continues: Causes and conflicts / George Martin. 1970.
    Includes bibliographical references and index.
    ISBN 0–8232–1738–8
    1. Association of the Bar of the City of New York—History.
I. Martin, George Whitney.   Causes and conflicts.   II. Title.
KF334.N4A8452   1997
340'.06'07471—dc21   96-53943
                                                          CIP

Printed in the United States of America

To Dean Howard A. Glickstein
and my colleagues on the Touro Law Faculty
who share with the City Bar the belief that
"if our heart is in the profession,
our soul is in *pro bono* work"

Contents

Illustrations follow page 88.

Foreword

by Michael A. Cardozo

Twenty-five years have elapsed since *Causes and Conflicts*, the centennial history of the Association, was published in 1970, a period that has seen sweeping social change at the Association of the Bar of the City of New York.

Mirroring the legal profession itself, membership has grown in absolute numbers and has become significantly more diverse in gender, ethnicity, and perspective. In rapid succession, in 1990 and 1994, the Association elected as its president its first African-American and its first woman. The Thurgood Marshall Summer Law Internship Program was established to provide paying summer jobs in legal environments for inner-city high school students. "Glass Ceilings and Open Doors: Women's Advancement in the Profession," a study commissioned by the Committee on Women in the Profession, was issued in September 1995.

With the establishment of the Robert B. McKay Community Outreach Law Program in 1987, the Association enhanced its tradition of public service. Community Outreach trains and supports volunteers who provide free legal services to those who need it most. A Community Outreach volunteer might mediate a child-custody dispute, advocate for a person with cancer facing employment discrimination, represent an individual in immigration proceedings, or participate in a clinic to help the homeless.

The Monday Night Legal Advisory Workshop, run by the Young Lawyers Committee, offers half-hour consultations to New Yorkers who cannot afford a lawyer. Our Legal Referral Service handles more than 100,000 calls each year from individuals needing information and referrals. In response to the economic downturn of the 1980s and 1990s, the Lawyers in Transition Program was established to provide advice and support to lawyers who are unemployed or underemployed.

We now have more than 180 committees that continue to perform valuable public service, issuing thoughtful and carefully researched reports to influence public policy. Case in point: the Judiciary Committee, one of the three original Association committees, which strives to uphold the quality of the judiciary through its evaluation of candidates for the bench, and which, from its inception, has been committed to maximizing the quality of the judiciary.

The Association's continuing efforts in this regard—from leading the successful effort in the 1970s to effect merit selection for judges of the New York Court of Appeals to opposing, in 1987, the nomination of Robert Bork to the Supreme Court of the United States—are chronicled in the pages that follow.

The Association was founded in 1870 to confront a crisis of confidence in the judiciary and to seek the removal of corrupt judges. Today we are faced with another crisis affecting the courts, but this time it is not corruption on or off the bench; it is a crisis caused by some in the media and some politicians insisting that cases be decided in accordance with public opinion polls and demanding that judges be removed from the bench because of disagreement with their decisions. As an Association we have been and must continue to be vigilant in this area, issuing reports and speaking out to the media about the importance of the independence of the judiciary.

Our landmark House will receive a special present as it celebrates its 100th anniversary this year—a significant addition and renovation that will include sorely needed offices and a training facility for the Community Outreach program. Though the building will change physically, the spirit and traditions it shelters will remain the same.

In *"Making Sure We Are True to Our Founders,"* Professor Jeffrey Morris provides an excellent account of the Association's growth and development during the first part of its second century. The publication of this volume would not have been possible without the generosity of Fordham University School of Law and its outstanding Dean, and former Association President, John D. Feerick.

At the 125th Anniversary Celebration of the Association held in September 1995, my immediate predecessor, Barbara Paul Robinson, remarked that if Central Park could be called the lungs of New York, then the Association should be called its conscience. As we

head toward the third millennium, that responsibility is more important than ever. Long-established institutions run the risk of basking
in tradition and past accomplishments, and sometimes have a tendency to rest on their laurels. We can ill afford to do that. Even
greater than the debt we owe to our founders is the responsibility we
owe to those who will follow. We must expand and remold tradition
to the temper of the times. We owe it to our predecessors, to our
descendants, and to ourselves.

Preface

In the spring of 1994, I was invited to write a history of the Association of the Bar of the City of New York from the time of its centennial (1970) to its 125th anniversary. I was promised editorial independence as well as access to persons and documents. I accepted the invitation with some reluctance—reluctance stemming not from a lack of respect for the nation's oldest and most distinguished bar association, but rather from doubt that there was a story to tell and, if there was a story, whether it was possible to tell it in a way that would be interesting to the reader.

That there was a story to tell became evident early in my work. An association of lawyers which had at the time of its centennial a deserved reputation for service to profession, community, and nation, but also a not undeserved reputation as the stronghold of male, WASP (and often starchy) Wall Street lawyers, would be transformed within a generation. Without sacrificing the most important virtues it had demonstrated during its first century, the Association became much more diverse and developed new roles, thus maintaining its role as the standard bearer of the profession. During its first century, the Association had been distinguished for the capacity of its leaders and members to "leave its clients at the door." On occasion, it had spoken up strongly on the political process and quality in the courts. It had produced a body of committee reports which had often proven extremely valuable for governmental decision-makers.

During the following twenty-five years the City Bar would, without sacrificing the virtues demonstrated during its first century, become a vastly more inclusive organization, speak out on urgent local, state, and national issues even more frequently than before, and greatly enlarge its mission of providing legal services to the less fortunate. The Association of the Bar of the City of New York, like other bar associations, had long been involved in some such efforts, but the magnitude and effectiveness of City Bar's involvement increased dramatically between 1970 and 1995. At first, the Association sought to increase the efforts of law firms and lawyers by providing a structure to stimulate those efforts. But, observing that that was not enough, the Association became directly involved in the provision of legal services to the homeless, the immigrant, the welfare recipient, the AIDS patient, and other communities desperately needing legal assistance. It has spawned program after program representing the "helping and healing" side of the law.

Not only has the Association become a role model for other bar associations in directly providing legal services for the poor, but it has done so by becoming vastly more inclusive—of Jews and Catholics, minorities, women, younger and elder lawyers, lesbian and gay lawyers, and the physically disabled—not just welcoming them as members, but by offering them positions of leadership, the City Bar has also demonstrated how such change can occur without convulsion. During a time when the nation's politics have become more fragmented, the City Bar has stood out for its tolerance of diversity.

That, in essence, is the story to be told. Whether it has been told well is for the reader to determine. This book begins with a description of some of the most important themes of the first hundred years of the Association. In this, the author has benefited greatly from George Martin's *Causes and Conflicts: The Centennial History of the Association of the Bar of the City of New York*. It has, however, been necessary to describe some events and trends of the 1960s to which Martin paid little attention (for their significance might not then have been clear). They are related here for presaging and influencing the developments between 1970 and 1995. Beyond this, although charged with writing the history of the Association during its fifth quarter-of-a-century, I found it necessary to begin the detailed part of the book not in 1970, but in 1968. The reason for this is simple: the City Bar president who began his service that year, Francis T. P. Plimpton, was the single most important figure in the transformation of the Association. By his willingness to speak out on great issues—issues whose focus was not narrowly limited to the profession or to judicial administration—during a period of great national division, Plimpton not only revived what the Association had been at its best, but attracted to it many young lawyers who otherwise might not have involved themselves in such a quintessentially "Establishment" organization. They contributed importantly to the remarkable transformation of the organization.

Beginning with Plimpton's presidency, there are seven chapters, each but the last dealing with a four-year period (the terms of two City Bar Presidents). The last of these presidencies, that of Barbara Paul Robinson, was only half over at the time of the commemoration of the 125th anniversary and is, therefore, not fully treated. Undoubtedly, the format of this book and its emphases understate the contributions of the committees of the City Bar to technical reform of the law and change in judicial administration. Not only would full justice to the contributions of the now 180 committees of the Association have required a very much longer book, but it might have yielded a book no one would have wanted to read. I have been conscious of the great significance of the work of the committees to the contributions of the Association and have attempted not only to discuss some of the more influential committee reports of the period, but also to suggest through example the richness of the committee work.

This book is based in part upon the publications of the Association, most particularly the *Record of the Association of the Bar of the City of New York*, a journal that has been published seven to nine times a year, and *44th Street Notes*, a newsletter published almost every month of the year since March 1986. The author has also studied unpublished papers of the Association, including the minutes of the stated meetings and committee reports not published in the record. In addition, I have drawn upon the scrapbooks of newspaper clippings for the years 1970 to 1979, scrapbooks which can be found in the Association's distinguished library, and upon the summaries of newspaper coverage which have been produced monthly since 1986 by the office of the Executive Secretary for dissemination to the Executive Committee.

This book could not have been written without the interviews I undertook of all living presidents of the Association going back to 1962 and all living chairpersons of the Executive Committee save two going back to 1968. Many of these men and women also provided me with extremely useful published and unpublished materials. I also spoke at length with the Executive Secretary of the Association and its General Counsel and have been the beneficiary of their enormous assistance.

This project could not have been carried through without the assistance of Seth Muraskin, a 1995 graduate of the Touro Law Center (and now a member of the New York Bar and of the City Bar), who indefatigably, speedily, and perspicaciously sifted enormous amounts of information at the Association. The judgments I made as to the significance of developments, judgments for which I am solely responsible, could not as a practical matter have been made without Seth's guidance. I also have been assisted by Seth's successor as research assistant, Donna McElhinney, who gave the book a thorough critical reading. Melissa Halili, Executive Assistant to the Executive Secretary of the Association, handled the very complicated scheduling of interviews, as well as tracking down innumerable amounts of obscure materials for Seth and me, cheerfully, intelligently, and efficiently. She eased our work and helped make it a pleasure. Howard A. Glickstein, Dean of the Touro Law Center, not only generously adjusted my schedule in such a way that I was able to handle other scholarly obligations and thereby take on and complete this project, but also has been a source of great encouragement and personal strength for me. As with my other recent writings, I am under an enormous debt to the Librarian of Touro Law School, Daniel P. Jordan, and to the staff of the Touro Library for innumerable instances of assistance—large and small. Finally, it should be made clear that it is only the author who ought to be held accountable for the judgments made in this work.

Jeffrey B. Morris

1

"No Bar Association I Know . . . Has Contributed More . . .": The City Bar on the Eve of Its Centennial

INTRODUCTION: WASHINGTON, MAY 1970

ON A SPRING MORNING in 1970 a chartered Penn-Central train from New York pulled into Union Station, Washington. Some 600 attorneys, many of them "Wall Street lawyers," got off the train and walked south five blocks. Passing the Supreme Court of the United States and arriving at the Capitol, they massed on the Capitol steps, joined by hundreds of others who had flown, driven, or taken the bus from New York, as well as colleagues from Philadelphia and the District of Columbia. New York's two senators, Jacob K. Javits and Charles Goodell, addressed the group. Then, the 1,200 attorneys,* "well-barbered, well-tailored and well-prepared" (with briefing forms, background exhibits, and a forty-nine–page position paper on the legal status of the Vietnam War), divided into 150 teams and fanned out through Washington to meet with members of Congress and officials of the Nixon Administration. What was happening was most unusual even at a time when the unusual was commonplace. These were not the proverbial scruffy anti-war demonstrators two Presidents loved to deride—the longhairs, young, idealistic, inexperienced. Most of this group was middle-aged and elderly. Many came from the nation's most prestigious law firms and, when they were on the job, represented some of America's biggest corporations and institutions. To the extent the lawyers had a leader, it was Francis T.

*Estimates vary from 650 to 1,200 lawyers.

P. Plimpton, president of the nation's oldest incorporated bar association and among its most distinguished, The Association of the Bar of the City of New York. The Association was not a formal sponsor of the trip to Washington, but many of those who went to Washington had rallied in the Association's House the night before. A full-page advertisement appearing in the *The New York Times* the day of the "march" employed the Association's name in ¾-inch letters across the page. Among those who participated that day were three of the Association's next four presidents—Bernard Botein, Orville Schell, and Adrian DeWind—as well as many of its future leaders.

A new chapter had begun in the life of this hundred-year–old organization. That The Association of the Bar of the City of New York would commit itself on issues of national importance was worthy of remark, but that had occurred at other times. What the event of May 20, 1970, signaled was not just, in the argot of the 1960s, that the hundred-year–old organization could still be "relevant," but also that the Association would be able to make the transition from a clubby, "WASPy," white-shoe organization to one vastly more inclusive without diminishing its integrity or the excellence of its work. As it reached its centennial, the City Bar would become more vigorous and active than ever before, defining new roles for bar associations throughout the nation.

AN ELITIST ORGANIZATION

Commemorating its centennial in 1970, not only was The Association of the Bar of the City of New York the most prestigious state or local bar association in the nation, but to many it had a far more illustrious history than the American Bar Association. The prestige of the Association was the result of its location in New York, the legal capital of the nation; the reputation of its leaders, among whom had been numbered William T. Evarts, Elihu Root, and Charles Evans Hughes; and, even more, because it had always aimed much higher than just being a trade association, had often succeeded, and, on at least several great occasions, had met the highest expectations of its founders.

Roscoe Pound had once assured the American Bar Association that it was not "the same sort of thing as a retail grocers' association,"[1] but that indeed was what most American bar associations were when Pound had written and what they continued to be in 1970. Most bar associations existed to provide services for their members—a library, a journal (usually dealing with parochial or antiquarian concerns), and a place to socialize and to drink in professional self-satisfaction—and most attended to a narrow spectrum of professional concerns: professional ethics and discipline, reform in judicial administration, the selection of judges, and the correctional system. They were professionally directed, not public-spirited, working to see that other professions did not infringe upon the "turf" of attorneys and attempting to counter perennial hostile sentiments about lawyers.

Although never ignoring these functions completely, The Association of the Bar of the City of New York had always been a bit different. It never had seen itself as just an Association to serve its members. The City Bar had been formed during the "Gilded Age" as a municipal watchdog organization to clean up municipal politics and clean out corrupt courts, and it had succeeded, making a major contribution to routing the Tweed ring and forcing corrupt judges off the bench. Although it could boast of many smaller achievements, the only ones in the history of the Association comparable to those of the early days were its dramatic stand in 1919, during a time of national political intolerance, against the expulsion of Socialist members from the New York State Assembly and the measured use of its resources to oppose McCarthyism a generation and a half later.

During the first hundred years, the Association had been led by extremely successful Wall Street lawyers who represented great concentrations of wealth, but who felt a particular responsibility for the moral order of the profession and the legitimacy of the legal system. Through its activities the Association became identified with legal reform and professional regulation, thereby imbuing its initiatives with considerable moral force. If its leaders, as lawyers, represented great concentrations of wealth, in their public service activities they sought to mediate between private acquisitiveness and re-distributive efforts, while struggling to bring the influence of lawyers at their best to bear on civic issues. Thus, the Association offered its facilities not only for technical legal reforms, but for broader social concerns as well, while the work of its committees, generally not infected with the interests of its members' clients, was marked by a high standard of civic duty. Because many of its leaders also possessed a strong social conscience, the City Bar, more than most bar associations, had recognized its obligations to the poor and the underdog.[2]

Yet, at the time of the centennial, there were many who felt that the Association was still an elitist organization, run like a private club. A prospective member had to be sponsored by a current member and then have separate interviews with members of the Admissions Committee. Although that committee spent more time dining than it did in working and very few applicants were ever formally black-balled, the procedure discouraged many from applying. The Association was not seen as particularly hospitable by ethnic Catholics, African-Americans, lawyers from small firms, and women. The leaders were men from the large Wall Street law firms, who had attended the same elite colleges and law schools (often the same private schools as well), then succeeded in what was then the clubby atmosphere of Wall Street.[3] The large firms could essentially place their members where they wanted on the committees. There had been an Irish Catholic president of the Association and two Jewish presidents, but these were men who had been assimilated into the dominant WASP culture.

A few men could caucus and produce the next president, sometimes someone who had demonstrated little more than a bare interest in the Association. The Executive Committee was "all powerful and self-perpetuating." The monthly meetings were spent at formal dinners at the Century Club, beginning with cocktails at 4:30 in the afternoon and lasting until the middle of the evening.

Such social aristocracy would have seemed outdated after the Second World War. An Association attempting to run itself that way could not have survived the 1960s and 1970s in good shape. Yet, such a social oligarchy should not be condemned out-of-hand. Even if the Wall Street firms could put pretty much whom they wanted on the Association's committees, those people were socialized into an Association with integrity and a professional conscience. Men who lived by the highest ethical and moral standards—the Charles Evans

Hugheses and Henry L. Stimsons—had been attracted to the Association as they had been attracted to the nation's public service. Whatever the limitations of the City Bar during its first century, it had been socially concerned. Surely, its outlook had been several thousand years more progressive than the American Bar Association, which had opposed the Child Labor Amendment and the U.N. Genocide Convention, strongly commended the House Un-American Activities Committee in the 1950s for its adherence to due process, and supported congressional legislation to override Supreme Court decisions expanding individual liberty.[4]

CHANGE IN THE 1960S

Important changes could be seen in the Association in the years just before the centennial—not in its internal style, but in the increased depth of social commitment. That the Association was becoming a different institution was apparent on the night of April 21, 1964, when Martin Luther King, Jr., making his first address to any American bar association, spoke at the House on "The Civil Rights Struggle in the United States Today." The Association's hall then held 650, and there was room for another 500 or 600 in the rest of the building. The day after the meeting had been announced in *The New York Law Journal*, there were 1,800 requests for reservations. The very next day, there were 4,000 requests (the total membership of the City Bar at the time was 8,000), and the Association had to run a notice in the law journal discouraging further reservations.[5]

On the 21st, 1,500 attended. King began by telling his audience that "the road to freedom is now a highway because lawyers throughout the land, yesterday and today, have helped clear the obstructions, have helped eliminate roadblocks, by their selfless, courageous espousal of difficult and unpopular causes." To an audience consisting mostly of lawyers, King explained his approach to violating the law:

We . . . believe that he who openly disobeys a law, a law that conscience tells him is unjust, and then willingly accepts the penalty, gives evidence thereby that he belongs in jail until it is changed. Our appeal is to the conscience.[6]

And, in words that anticipated his martyrdom just four years later, King preached that:

> Before the victory is won, some more will have to go to jail; before the victory is won, some will have to get scarred up a bit; before the victory is won, some will be misunderstood and called bad names. Before the victory is won, maybe somebody else will face physical death, but if physical death is the price that some must pay to free their children and their white brothers from a permanent death of the spirit, then nothing can be more redemptive.[7]

Even before King's appearance, the leaders of the Association had left little doubt where they stood on the greatest issue then facing the nation. The most influential leader of the Association in the postwar era, Harrison Tweed, was serving as co-chair of the Lawyers' Committee on Civil Rights Under Law, created as the result of the call of President John F. Kennedy on June 21, 1963.[8] At Tweed's request, the president of the Association, then Herbert Brownell, had created the Special Committee for Civil Rights Under Law. Francis E. Rivers, a former judge of the Civil Court and an African-American, was named to chair the committee whose mission was to study the effectiveness of federal procedural remedies in protecting civil rights.[9] Whitney North Seymour, J. Lee Rankin, Sam Rosenman, Lloyd K. Garrison, and Robert L. Carter were among the committee's members. Berl I. Bernard, an expert in the field, was chosen as staff director.

At the same time, the Association's Committee on Federal Legislation gave strong support to the civil rights legislation pending in the Congress, the passage of which, at least prior to the assassination of President Kennedy, was in doubt. The committee, which was chaired by Fred N. Fishman and included Louis Craco and Robert Kaufman as members, strongly endorsed the objectives of the legislation and explained why the law would be constitutional under both the Commerce Clause and the Fourteenth Amendment. It was "manifestly reasonable," the committee stated in its report, for Congress to make findings that discrimination in public accommodations burdens and obstructs interstate commerce. "Congress is not limited under the Commerce Clause by the size or impact on commerce of any particular enterprise subjected to regulation," the committee reported; it is "the aggregate impact on commerce of any particular enterprise subjected to regulation" that matters.[10] On August 28, 1963, the day that 250,000 Americans rallied at the Lincoln Memorial on behalf of the proposed civil rights legislation, *The New York Times* ran an editorial referring to the report of the committee.

Support for the civil rights bill and for civil rights was demonstrated by the Association in other ways in the year between the introduction of the legislation by the Administration in June 1963 and its enactment on July 2, 1964. On October 20, 1963, Chief Justice Earl Warren, who had dropped out of the American Bar Association in the 1950s because of the political positions it was taking as well as the slights to his office, came to the House to accept honorary membership. While "Impeach Earl Warren" picketers were out in full force on 44th Street, a huge crowd of members of the Association entered through the 43rd Street doors. Governor Nelson Rockefeller and Mayor Robert Wagner greeted the Chief Justice formally. Warren then had this to say of the Association:

> There is no Bar Association I know in this country or any other that has contributed more to legal history or to the jurisprudence of our country than this great Association. I think that it is interested in the very fundamentals of the legal profession and of our society when it does things it has been doing in recent years. . . . And so I embrace the opportunity to be among this group, to be one of the fellowship.[11]

In February 1964, while the civil rights bill was pending, a symposium was held at the House on civil rights litigation at which Thurgood Marshall, Jack Greenberg, and Robert McKay spoke.[12] In May 1964, the Committee on Federal Legislation and the Committee on Labor and Social Security Legislation together "strongly endorse[d] the concept of equal employment opportunity" embodied in each of the major bills pending in the Congress and stated that they were validly founded on the Commerce Clause.[13] Then, at its May meeting, the Executive Committee adopted a resolution recording its "emphatic view that it [the pending bill] is urgently needed and should be enacted." "This bill," the committee wrote, "tests whether our federal institutions can and will give valid and effective expression to our national conscience."[14] At the stated meeting of December 8, 1964, after the agenda was disposed of, Harrison Tweed chaired a panel of civil rights lawyers who had been in Mississippi the previous summer.[15]

The following year, five weeks after the Selma-to-Montgomery March had begun and less than one month after Lyndon Johnson had given a televised speech endorsing legislation to protect voting rights, the Committees on Federal Legislation and on the Bill of Rights reported, stating: "We conclude that a new statute to enforce the Fifteenth Amendment to the Constitution is urgently required because [t]he history of the development of Negro Voting Rights since the ratification of the Fourteenth Amendment in 1870 has been replete with constant efforts, both simple and sophisticated, to circumvent its basic purpose." "No constitutional objection could be sustained against the bill," the committees concluded, "[s]ince Congress may determine the means to attack the evil of discrimination in voting."[16] A year later, the Committee on Federal Legislation supported another civil rights bill, the one that became the Fair Housing Act, but urged its strengthening.[17]

The growing liberal cast of the Association in the 1960s can be seen in positions taken in areas other than civil rights. In 1965, the Committee on Federal Legislation strongly opposed a constitutional amendment to take reapportionment cases away from the Supreme Court.[18] The same year, the Committees on Administrative Law and on Municipal Affairs recommended the creation of a civilian review board in the New York City Police Department.[19] Several years later, the Committee on Medicine and Law sought enactment by the New York State Legislature of a liberalized abortion law,[20] while the Special Committee on Problems of Law Enforcement opposed the adoption by the legislature of stop-and-frisk and no-knock laws.[21]

Even though it does not bear on the growing liberal cast of the

Association, brief mention ought be made of some other work of committees in the mid-1960s, the impact of which could not have been clear at the time George Martin wrote his centennial history, *Causes and Conflicts*.[22] The study of the subject of privacy by the Special Committee on Science and Law, chaired by Oscar Ruebhausen, stimulated interdisciplinary seminars and convention panels, a study by the federal government, and new federal contracting procedures. The committee commissioned the seminal modern work on the subject, Alan F. Westin's *Privacy and Freedom*.[23]

The problem of the role of the press in criminal trials had to be reexamined in the 1960s as a result of several United States Supreme Court decisions. The ABA appointed a committee chaired by Judge Paul Reardon, while the Association appointed the Special Committee on Radio, Television, and the Administration of Justice, chaired by Judge Harold J. Medina.[24] The Medina Committee was much friendlier to the media than the Reardon Committee, concluding that courts should not be given additional contempt powers to fine or imprison members of the news media or the police for leaks. It also recommended a voluntary code for police and other law enforcement officials and urged the strengthening of the Canons of Professional Ethics to curb the tendency of some lawyers to try their cases in the media. Both reports received considerable attention and influenced jurisprudential developments in the 1970s.

There were several significant legislative successes in the 1960s. The Committee on Federal Legislation was one of the most influential voices in the successful effort that produced a constitutional amendment dealing with the problems of Presidential inability and a vacancy in the office of Vice President.[25] The committee was less successful in its support for a constitutional amendment to abolish the Electoral College.[26] In the mid-1960s a bill drafted by the Special Committee on the Study of Commitment Procedures to Amend New York State's Mental Hygiene Law regarding the admission, retention, and discharge of patients in psychiatric institutions became law. In addition, the work of the Association greatly influenced the reform of the state's archaic divorce laws.[27]

THE ASSOCIATION ON THE EVE OF ITS CENTENNIAL

On the eve of its centennial the Association had just under 10,000 members. Leadership was divided among the president, the Executive Secretary, and the committees. Unlike those of professional organizations, the president of the City Bar served not a one-year term, but for two years. Throughout the first hundred years the presidency had always been held by partners in large law firms (with the exception of Dean Russell Niles of New York University Law School, president 1966–68). The Special Committee on the Second Century explained why:

> It is clear that the only lawyers who can afford to serve are those who have ample private means or who are associated with a firm or corporation or institution which is prepared to continue paying them, while they are spending most of their time on Association affairs.[28]

Although the president did not have an office in the House until the presidency of Sam Rosenman (1964–66), the Association was "president-driven" in many respects. Besides the ceremonial duties which each president performed, he was expected to appoint the chairs of committees and committee members, especially if there was a need to achieve diversity of viewpoint, and to monitor the work of the committees. In this period, it was still possible for the president to attend at least one meeting of each committee every year. If most of the first year in office was spent getting to know the staff and committee chairmen and grasping the machinery of the Association, by the second year the president could shape the office. The presidency offered its incumbent a magnificent platform from which to be heard and the capacity to create new committees or reshape old ones in order to achieve important substantive goals.

In 1970, the Association had five vice presidents who generally served two to three years with little in the way of duties or responsibilities. Its secretary (an *ex officio* member of the Executive Committee) was by tradition under thirty-five years old and expected to bring to that committee "the energy and viewpoint of [relative] youth."[29] There was also a treasurer who traditionally served for four years and who was expected to fulfill the responsibilities usually given to treasurers.

On the other hand, the office of Executive Secretary was quite important. The Executive Secretary in 1970 was Paul B. De Witt, who had held the office since its creation in 1945. He would continue to serve until 1979, retiring after serving under a total of seventeen presidents. De Witt had attended the University of Iowa and Harvard, where he received his second masters degree, and the University of Michigan Law School. Before the Second World War, De Witt had been active with the Iowa Bar Association and had served as reporter for the rules committee of the Iowa Supreme Court. After the war, Harrison Tweed brought him to the Association. Tremendously dedicated and effective, articulate, and opinionated, De Witt was omnipresent. He served as executive assistant to the president, resource person and coordinator to the committees, editor of *The Record*, and public relations officer. Sixty years old in the centennial year, De Witt was the first source of information about the Association's activities and the principal coordinator of those activities. He exerted influence over Association policy and committee appointments, among other areas. He had, Merrell Clark recalled, "a special gift for being the prime mover of a project while remaining almost invisible in the background."[30] De Witt had the distinct talent of getting prima donnas to work well together. He was also an elitist who put a premium upon the Association's "looking sharp and professional and expensive."[31] Russell Niles put it gracefully:

> One of Paul's strong points was style. He rather believed in elegance.
> The publications of the Association during his administration had style.
> He wanted the decor, the service, the ambience of the House of the
> Association to be of high quality. He believed in the grand manner.[32]

If De Witt's interest in every aspect of the Association was total, it should, nevertheless, be pointed out that the library of the Association and the Grievance Committee functioned semi-autonomously, while the House had an Administrative Manager who reported not to De Witt, but to the House Committee.

The principal work of the Association was done by its committees.

At the time of the centennial, there were about eighty committees. The chairs, holding their positions for three-year terms, were selected by the president, assisted by the Executive Secretary. The committees varied in size from four to forty-five, but averaged about eighteen members. During the next quarter-of-a-century, the number of committees would more than double, and the average size increase to thirty-one.

Three committees had a special status under the Association's bylaws. The Committees on State Legislation, on Federal Legislation, and on Criminal Courts, Law and Procedure could announce positions as being that of the Association. The Committees on Federal Legislation and State Legislation produced very different products. The Committee on Federal Legislation, dealing primarily with issues concerning the workings of the federal system and the interplay between the federal system and individual liberties, had become a national voice when it spoke on such matters. These were substantive matters of important policy significance. Because the New York State Legislature had limited staff assistance, the Committee on State Legislation which reviewed hundreds of bills annually was, by the time of the centennial, concerned more with form than with substance.[33] When passing on qualifications of judicial candidates, the Committee on the Judiciary also spoke for the Association. The Committee on Professional and Judicial Ethics did so as well, when providing declaratory judgments on questions of ethical conduct.[34] The Grievance Committee was largely responsible for the prosecution of professional disciplinary matters for most of New York City (Brooklyn matters were handled by the local bar there), bringing attorneys formally before the Appellate Division. Its reputation was also national, and its work was viewed as "among the most important tasks of the Association."[35]

On the eve of the centennial, the library continued to be one of the great jewels of the Association. With 359,365 volumes as of April 30, 1970, and a valuable collection of records and briefs, it was the largest bar library in the country.[36] If it was one of the great attractions of the Association, the library was also a large item in its budget and posed perennial problems of storage.

The Record of the Association, first published in 1946, consisted of nine issues a year in 1970, annually totaling around 850 pages. *The Record* was a respectable and respected law journal. In every issue, there were a few pages devoted to the current activities of the Association. Leading articles were usually based on lectures given at the House by distinguished figures in the law. Additionally, important and timely committee reports were printed in *The Record*. Finally, many issues contained a bibliography on a specialized topic prepared by the librarian. Virtually all its editorial work was done by Paul De Witt.[37] The Association also published a yearbook, containing the constitution and bylaws and a listing of the entire membership of the Association, as well as a list of the members of each committee. There was also an annual book of memorials. In addition, collections of the reports of the Committee on State Legislation, the Committee on Criminal Courts, and the Committee on Federal Legislation were issued annually.[38]

Occasionally, important studies of the committees were published as books. Among the most widely read in the 1960s were *Conflict of Interest and Federal Service* (Harvard University Press, 1960), *Mental Illness and Due Process* (Cornell University Press, 1962); *Freedom of the Press and Fair Trial* (Columbia University Press, 1967); and *Privacy and Freedom* (Athenaeum, 1967).

Although the Association had never attempted to rival the Practising Law Institute in offering continuing legal education, it did provide its members and the general public with a rich program of lectures spiked with an occasional forum. The most prestigious of the lectures was the Benjamin N. Cardozo Lecture, which for more than thirty years had been given by men of the caliber of Robert Jackson (1944), Felix Frankfurter (1946), Charles Wyzanski (1952), and Henry J. Friendly (1964). Some of the lectures in that series had become classics and been widely republished.

At the time of the centennial, the financial position of the Association was relatively good. Its assets included the House, the adjoining Bar Building, and an endowment of several million dollars. Most of its revenues came from dues, but the Association also received rent payments from the Bar Building and interest from its endowment. Its financial position would worsen appreciably during the sharp inflation of the 1970s.[39]

If, at the time of the hundredth anniversary of its birth, the Association's greatest strength was its reputation for the high quality and neutrality of the work of its committees and its integrity, probably its greatest weakness was the distance it had traditionally kept from other organizations that shared some of the same concerns—bar groups and civic organizations—and the way it was perceived by some of them. In 1974, the Special Committee on the Second Century addressed the first failing this way:

> The Association's relationship toward other organizations related to its field of interest has presented a challenge not satisfactorily met in the first century. Whether stemming from attitudes of self-imposed uniqueness or conscious timidity in restricting its purposes to naked legal issues divorced from judgmental public policy issues which should properly emanate from others, the result has been that the Association has not developed an involved, integrated relationship with other organizations which seem to be clearly related to many of its significant purposes.[40]

The Association also was perceived by the borough bar associations and many of their members and by many municipal politicians, especially those from the outer boroughs, as patrician in outlook, unconcerned about and unsympathetic to the interests of the outer boroughs, and politically unrealistic in many of its stands.

*   *   *

Instead of dying of hardening of the arteries around the time it commemorated its centennial, The Association of the Bar of the City of New York became infused with new vigor. In twenty-five years the membership would grow from 9,924 to more than 20,000. Committees also grew in number and members. Inclusiveness replaced exclusivity. A membership of middle-aged to elderly male WASP Wall Street lawyers became much more heterogeneous. Women, Jews, ethnic Catholics, African-Americans, Hispanic-Americans, Asian-Americans, academic, government lawyers, public defenders, lawyers from smaller firms, and young lawyers joined in large numbers. There was a deliberate and successful attempt to accelerate these new members into leadership positions. While retaining some of its own style—and its building—the Association became, as Professor Beatrice S. Frank put it, "user friendly."[41] Not the least of the reasons for this has been the influence of Fern Schair, who, in 1982, became the third Executive Secretary. As influential in her way as Paul De Witt was, she has pushed the Association to be more inclusive and warmer and to undertake directly many more activities.

With a more heterogeneous membership, the Association has greatly increased the range of its activities, reaching out to practitioners far more than ever before by undertaking such programs as assisting out-of-work lawyers and attorney substance-abusers. Paralleling its efforts toward inclusion within have been its efforts to increase the hiring of minority attorneys on Wall Street and to encourage their retention and promotion.

But the most dramatic change in the work of the Association has been its involvement in the "helping and the healing side of the law,"[42] spawning programs to address the problems of the homeless, immigrants, welfare recipients, tenants, and other groups.

Furthermore, in sharp contrast to its first hundred years, the Association has sought out other groups—bar associations, smaller and less institutionalized groups of lawyers, and "good government" groups—to make its views more effective through coalition building.

*   *   *

To these developments—inclusiveness within and without the Association, vigor and range of activities, warmth and the direct provision of *pro bono* services—and others, we now turn.

NOTES

1. Quoted in Deborah L. Rohde, "Why the ABA Bothers: A Functional Perspective on Professional Codes," *Texas Law Review*, 59 (1991), 689.

2. Michael L. Powell, *From Patrician to Professional Elite: The Transformation of the New York City Bar Asssociation* (New York: Russell Sage Foundation, 1988), pp. 18, 231, 240; Anthony Lewis, review of George Martin, *Causes and Conflicts*, *American Bar Association Journal*, 56 (May 1970), 478 ; interview with John D. Feerick, February 21, 1995.

3. Interviews with George G. Gallantz, February 24, 1995; Michael A. Cardozo,

February 21, 1995; Beatrice S. Frank, February 16, 1995; M. Bernard Aidinoff, March 9, 1995; and Oscar M. Ruebhausen, March 21, 1995.

4. Mark Green, "The ABA as Trade Association," in *Verdicts on Lawyers*, ed. Ralph Nader and Mark J. Green (New York: Thomas Y. Crowell, 1976), p. 5; John R. Schmidhauser and Larry L. Berg, "The American Bar Association and the Human Rights Conventions: The Political Significance of Private Professional Associations," *Social Research*, 38 (1971), 362, 382–83.

5. Samuel Rosenman, "Introductory Remarks to Martin Luther King, 'The Civil Rights Struggle in the United States Today,'" *The Record*, 20 (1965), Supplement, p. 3.

6. Martin Luther King, "The Civil Rights Struggle in the United States Today," ibid., pp. 3, 5, 6.

7. Ibid., p. 18. King's address was republished in a supplement to *The Record* of June 1968, along with the addresses given at the House on the night of his assassination; see *The Record*, 23 (June 1968), Supplement, p. 4.

8. *The Record*, 19 (March 1964), 282.

9. Ibid., 129–31.

10. Committee on Federal Legislation, "Proposed Federal Civil Rights Laws Relating to Public Accommodations," *The Record*, 18 (1963), 609, 596, 600.

11. Quoted in Tribute of J. Lee Rankin [to Earl Warren], *Memorial Vol. 1976*, p. 74. See also Herbert Brownell, *Advising Ike: The Memoirs of Attorney General Herbert Brownell* (Lawrence: University of Kansas Press, 1993), p. 348.

12. *The Record*, 19 (February 1964), 51.

13. Committee on Federal Legislation and Committee on Labor and Social Security Legislation, "Report on Proposed Federal Legislation Relating to Equal Employment Opportunity," *The Record*, 19 (May 1964), 230ff.

14. *The Record*, 19 (June 1964), 262–63.

15. *The Record*, 19 (December 1964), 518.

16. "Proposed Federal Legislation on Voting Rights," *The Record*, 20 (May 1965), 318, 317, 324.

17. Committee on Federal Legislation, "Report on Proposed Civil Rights Act of 1966," *The Record*, 22 (February 1967), 89.

18. "Report on Proposed Constitutional Amendments and Jurisdictional Limitations on Federal Courts with Respect to Apportionment of State Legislatures," *The Record*, 20 (April 1965), 229.

19. *The Record*, 20 (October 1965), 435–36.

20. Francis T. P. Plimpton, "Report of the President: 1968–1969," *The Record*, 24 (October 1969), 375, 403-404.

21. *The Record*, 19 (October 1968), 368.

22. George Martin, *Causes and Conflicts: The Centennial History of the Association of the Bar of the City of New York, 1870–1970* (Boston: Houghton Mifflin, 1970; repr. New York: Fordham University Press, 1997).

23. Alan F. Westin, *Privacy and Freedom* (New York: Athenaeum, 1967).

24. Special Committee on Radio, Television and the Administration of Justice, *Freedom of the Press and Fair Trial* (New York: Columbia University Press, 1967).

25. Committee on Federal Legislation, "Report on Problems of Presidential Inability and Vacancy in the Office of Vice President," *The Record*, 19 (June 1964), 311.

26. Committee on Federal Legislation, "Proposed Constitutional Amendment Abolishing Electoral College and Making Other Changes in Election of President and Vice President," *The Record*, 20 (October 1965), 503.

27. Powell, *From Patrician to Professional Elite*, pp. 215–19 (see above, note 2).

28. Special Committee on the Second Century, "Administration of the Association," *The Record*, 28 (November 1973), 715.

29. Ibid., 719.

30. Ibid., 721; Powell, *From Patrician to Professional Elite*, p. 89 (see above, note 2); Merrell E. Clark, Jr., "[Remarks on] Paul Burton De Witt, 1910–1985," *The Record*, 41 (January/February 1986), 50, 54, 55; interviews with Evan Davis, February 14, 1995; Adrian W. DeWind, February 2, 1995; Louis A. Craco, February 2, 1995; Sheldon Oliensis, February 17, 1995.

31. Interview with Evan Davis, February 14, 1995 (see above, note 30).

32. Russell O. Niles, "[Remarks on] Paul Burton De Witt," 50, 63, 64 (see above, note 30).

33. See Subcommittee Appointed by the Executive Committee, "Association's Legislative Activities," *The Record*, 38 (October 1983), 486.

34. Special Committee on the Second Century, "The Decision-Making Structure of the Association," *The Record*, 28 (February 1973), 102.

35. Special Committee on the Second Century, "The Committee on Grievances," *The Record*, 29 (October 1974), 563.

36. See Report of Library Committee, *The Record*, 25 (1970), Supplement No. 7, p. 50.

37. See Robert B. McKay, "Fortieth Anniversary of *The* Record," *The Record*, 41 (January–February 1986), 13.

38. Special Committee on the Second Century, "The Publications of the Association," *The Record*, 28 (December 1973), 828.

39. Special Committee on the Second Century, "The Financial Affairs of the Association," *The Record*, 29 (May-June 1974), 429.

40. Special Committee on the Second Century, "Relationship of the Association to the Community," *The Record*, 29 (January 1974), 69.

41. Interview with Beatrice S. Frank (see above, note 3).

42. The phrase is John D. Feerick's. Interview with John D. Feerick (see above, note 2).

2

"Militant Activists for the Constructive Reform of the Law": The Plimpton–Botein Years, 1968–72

FOR THE UNITED STATES, the years 1968 to 1972 were a time of profound national turmoil. The rule of law was threatened by assassinations, riots, political trials, and attempted government repression. For the Association of the Bar, these were extremely important years of transition. Opposition to the war in Indo-China and to the nomination of G. Harold Carswell to the Supreme Court of the United States by the City Bar while Francis T. P. Plimpton and Bernard Botein were president became emblematic examples of its willingness to take strong positions against what seemed to be the political mainstream. Within the Association those public stands helped to lessen the generational cleavages that harmed many institutions during these years. By reaching out to its younger members and by making structural changes in its governance, the City Bar began that process of inclusion which became the predominant theme of its fifth quarter-of-a-century.

THE PRESIDENTS: FRANCIS T. P. PLIMPTON AND BERNARD BOTEIN

Francis Plimpton, president from 1968 to 1970, was the preeminent figure in the transformation of the City Bar. With idealism, courage, and efficacy, Plimpton brought the Association face to face with burning issues (which many thought no business of the Association) and "jump-started" the organization to greater inclusiveness. A "white-shoe WASP" practicing with one of the bluest of blue-chip firms,

Plimpton was a difficult target for older, more conservative members. "Disarmingly conciliatory and naturally courteous," with "a large sense of humor," Plimpton looked to the future from the perspective of an elegant past.

Plimpton was the scion of an eminent Massachusetts family—dating back to John Plympton, who arrived in Roxbury in 1630, ultimately fell afoul of native Americans, and was burned at the stake. Born on East 33rd Street in 1900, Francis Plimpton was educated at Exeter, Amherst College, and the Harvard Law School, where one of his roommates was Adlai Stevenson. Neither man showed much enthusiasm for the law at Harvard. As a result of a recommendation Felix Frankfurter made to Walter Lippmann, Plimpton wrote editorials on legal subjects for the *New York World* while he was in law school. Hired by the firm of Root, Clark, Buckner, Howland & Ballantine upon graduation, Plimpton took over their Paris office from 1929 to 1931. When he returned to the United States, Plimpton was "lent" by Root, Clark to the Reconstruction Finance Corporation. But when he left the R.F.C. in 1933 Plimpton joined Debevoise & Stevenson (later Debevoise & Plimpton) as a partner. Eli Whitney Debevoise had been a classmate at Harvard, and Plimpton had known William Stevenson since private school.

At Debevoise, Plimpton was involved in the legal problems of railroad and public utilities reorganizations and the legal problems of financing under the Securities Act of 1933. Plimpton was best known as an attorney as a skilled writer of debentures, who could make them easier to read. His skill was such that Professor William L. Cary, later chairman of the Securities & Exchange Commission, said of Plimpton that: "He's the only person who can write an indenture in iambic pentameter."[1] Plimpton was also a member of the ABA Committee on Corporate Law which drafted the model corporation law, simplifying and modernizing it.

In 1961 Plimpton was appointed to the United States delegation to the United Nations at the behest of the U.S. Ambassador, Adlai Stevenson. There, Plimpton was assigned to the Special Political Committee and also was involved with the Budgetary and Legal Committees. He served as Stevenson's second-in-command, leaving in 1966 after Stevenson's death.

Francis Plimpton was a linguist, classical scholar, and tennis ace. He was a Harvard overseer and a trustee or a member of the boards of the New York Philharmonic, the Foreign Policy Association, the American-Italy Society, Roosevelt Hospital, the U.S. Trust Co., and the Metropolitan Museum of Art. (Not the least of his contributions to his city was to help secure the Temple of Dendur for the Metropolitan.) In the non-legal world, Francis Plimpton was best known as the father of George Plimpton, founder of the *Paris Review* and author of *Paper Lion.* If he was, as Herbert Brownell commented, someone "who wanted things done properly, a taskmaster and perfectionist—socially, educationally, family-wise," he was also, as Robert MacCrate recalls, a "delightful and a consummate diplomat."[2]

Plimpton had not been exceptionally active in the Association prior to his presidency, but as president his impact on the organization was enormous, possibly even "revolutionary," as Sheldon Oliensis suggested. "That was Francis," Oliensis said. "He thought that there was no issue on which the Association could not be heard."[3] Attractive to younger lawyers, he narrowed the fissures of the late 1960s. With courage and idealism, he brought the Association face to face with burning issues.[4]

Bernard Botein came from a different mold. The third Jewish president of the Association (after Louis Loeb and Sam Rosenman), Botein was born on the Lower East Side in 1900. He had worked his way through the City College of The City University of New York and Brooklyn. As an assistant district attorney, Botein had led the fight against ambulance-chasing lawyers. Named to the state Supreme Court by Governor Herbert Lehman, he was promoted to the Appellate Division, First Department by Governor Thomas Dewey, made its presiding justice by Governor Averell Harriman, and reappointed to that position by Governor Nelson Rockefeller. With the looks of an Old Testament prophet—dark, deep-set intense eyes beneath black, bushy brows and a shock of white hair—Botein was a man with a deep sense of social commitment and integrity. He had retired from the bench before his election to the presidency and was practicing law with the firm of Botein, Hays, Sklar & Hershberg.

Unlike Plimpton, Botein was shrewdly aware of New York City politics. He knew the local politicians, enjoyed mingling with them, and greatly enjoyed the game of politics. Like Plimpton, he was a good listener and had an excellent sense of humor, something he did not attempt to disguise in his annual reports as president. In his 1970–71 report, for example, he wrote:

> It is the tendency for Special Committees to become Standing Committees. It is therefore an event of true singularity to report the final report of the Committee on the Lawyers' Placement Bureau recommending its own termination.[5]

In the same report, he wrote:

> A study was also undertaken [by the Committee on Federal Legislation] on the proposed First Amendment Freedoms Act, concluding, on balance, that the First Amendment freedoms would be in somewhat better shape without the First Amendment Freedoms Act.[6]

As president, Botein did not attempt to lead the Association away from controversy. He supported efforts to work with the younger lawyers and created several important new committees, such as Sex and Law, which not only were attractive to younger lawyers, but involved the Association in new areas or in older areas in a new way. Botein died on February 3, 1974.

THE CENTENNIAL

The centennial was celebrated by publication of George Martin's *Causes and Conflicts: The Centennial History of the Association of the Bar of the City of New York*; symposia and art exhibitions; a great convocation at Lincoln Center; a dinner in the meeting hall, with a musical program consisting of songs from past productions of the Association as well as a new song composed in praise of Paul De Witt; a dinner for the Executive Committee attended by all former living and present members, at which Justice John Marshall Harlan, Merrell E. Clark, Jr., John Lindsay, and Whitney North Seymour spoke; a centennial ball held at the Metropolitan Museum of Art; and a dinner dance at the Waldorf-Astoria.

Among the symposia were one on forthcoming changes in legal education and the practice of law, with particular emphasis on public service activities of lawyers; and another on the decentralization of city government, at which Mayor John Lindsay spoke. Terry Lenzer, Director of Legal Services of the Organization for Economic Opportunity, who spoke at the former symposium, learned about his firing by President Richard Nixon immediately after leaving the podium in the meeting hall!

The House was the setting for art exhibits devoted to nineteenth-century New York and to contemporary graphic art on the subject of contemporary law and justice, which was displayed throughout the United States in such places as the Smithsonian, the Harvard Law School, and the Universities of Missouri and Arizona. The former exhibition was noncontroversial, but the latter, most of which was the work of younger artists, did not flatter contemporary American law. The exhibition certainly evoked the challenges to the rule of law at a time when the rule of law was under siege both by the opponents of the government and by the government itself. Francis Plimpton referred in his annual report to the exhibition as "certainly a lesson in the graphic vigor of the young artists of the day, and in the bitterness of their resentment against the conception of American law and justice."[7] Twenty-five years later, Merrell Clark remembered very clearly the art on the meeting room walls covered with blood, gore, and burning flags.[8] At the time, Plimpton wrote wryly in his annual report: "Virtually every exhibit made out American judges to be amalgams of Torquemada and Jeffreys of the bloody assizes and American trials to be *autos de fe* conducted in the dungeons of Chillon."[9]

The author of the centennial history, George Martin, was the son and grandson of members of the Association. Martin, too, was a lawyer, although he had given that up for a career as a fulltime writer. In a literary career of distinction, Martin is perhaps best known today for his works on opera.[10] Of his book on the Association, the first chapter of which was published in the April 1970 *Record*,[11] Louis Auchincloss, no small literary figure (and a member of the Association), wrote: "Martin has blazed a bright trail through very thick woods" and shown "that institutional history can be made an exciting thing."[12]

The great convocation commemorating the centennial took place on February 17, 1970, at Philharmonic Hall. Two thousand members and spouses attended. The program was preceded by a procession of some two hundred in academic gown or judicial robes with wives in formal dress. The principal speakers were Francis Plimpton, Mayor John Lindsay, Governor Nelson Rockefeller, and Chief Justice Warren Burger. The convocation was followed by a reception with food, drink, and strolling players.

Although he did not come to the ceremony, the American whose name is most associated with the meaning of the rule of law during the decade of the seventies, Richard Nixon, sent a telegram, stating:

> It is with many pleasant memories and with the pride of a onetime member that I send congratulations to the Association of the Bar of the City of New York on your centennial celebration. Nowhere does the Legal Profession play a more dynamic or indispensable role than in your city. Nowhere else are the needs as great. And no organization has given them as much prominence and constructive attention as your own. The distinction you have attained in the one hundred years of your eventful history is amply reflected in your creative leadership in metropolitan affairs as well as in the social conscience that inspires it. . . . It has been said that while a physician saves life, a lawyer is responsible for the society which makes life worth saving. Both individually and collectively your membership has always been ready to meet this responsibility. And in meeting it you have also been true to the highest traditions of our American heritage. . . .[13]

The speeches at the convocation went beyond mere platitudes. Plimpton, who began the program with a short address, stated that "law as an agency of social control is under attack as virtually never before." He charged the membership "to seek out and steadfastly fight for the changes that can and should be made to meet the just demands of today and tomorrow." "Let us," he said, "be militant activists, militant activists for the constructive reform of the law we were founded to promote."[14]

Lindsay, clearly with the Nixon Administration in mind, bluntly warned that the nation appeared headed "for a new period of repression more dangerous than at any time in years." He called for "faith in the system of open and free debate—and in full constitutional protection for those accused of crimes."[15]

Burger did not choose a subject of immediately hot controversy, but used the occasion to give an important substantive speech on penal reform. The Chief Justice pointed out that, "While we spend more and more each year to support our complex and, to me, unsatisfactory system of trials, appeals and retrials, increase our police forces and other mechanisms of protection, we exhibit an astonishing indifference to what happens to those who are sentenced."[16] In words as relevant today as they were in 1970, Burger argued:

> We could win *every* prosecution, convict *every* defendant, and imprison *every* guilty person, and still fail. We would fail because there must be two purposes, and the second purpose is not served by a perfect record on the first. Unless we succeed in both, we fail. To put a person behind walls and not change him is to win a battle and lose a war.[17]

The Association would disagree with Burger on a number of matters during his tenure as Chief Justice—matters such as qualifications for lawyers appearing in federal district court and the proposed National Court of Appeals—but always retained warm relations with the man it had made an honorary member.

THE ASSOCIATION AND THE INDO-CHINA WAR

The trip to Washington in May 1970 was the first time the Association had appeared to take a stand on the Vietnam War. A request to use the House for a meeting to rally support against the war, made in October 1969 by Manfred Ohrenstein, a state senator from Manhattan's West Side, had been turned down by Whitney North Seymour, chairman of the House Committee, because he feared that it might be construed as an Association activity. A second request was made for the use of the hall a few weeks later—this time to Plimpton—who agreed to it, in spite of sympathy in the Executive Committee for Seymour's position, on condition that the event was not an official bar association activity. There were, Plimpton thought, "legal issues involved," and that made it "perfectly proper to be held . . . in the Bar Association."[18]

Then came the announcement of April 30, 1970, that the United States had sent troops into neutral Cambodia. The national reaction was bitter. There were strikes on 286 college or university campuses. But it was not only the students who were upset. As Plimpton said, "The Presidential decision to invade Cambodia produced a galvanic shock in the New York legal community."[19]

Plimpton gave permission for the use of the meeting hall on May 19 for a convocation of lawyers recruited by Orville Schell, to be followed by the lobbying effort in Washington the next day. Plimpton saw the Washington trip as an effort "to try to prove to Congress that the better element of New York lawyers actually were against the bombing and invasion of Cambodia," which many thought "an errant violation of law."[20]

Plimpton had not until this time been a leader in the organization of the convocation of May 19 or the Washington trip (which actually was sponsored by the Lawyers Committee for Effective Action to End the Vietnam War and the Lawyers Convocation on Vietnam), although he had encouraged the convocation, agreed to take part in it, permitted the use of the meeting hall, and would be involved in the Washington lobbying. Plimpton indicated that neither the convocation nor the trip were to be labeled as Association activities. Nevertheless, he did not object to the full-page advertisement in *The New York Times* of May 17 which employed the Association's name in 3/4-inch letters across the page as the place for the meeting. That advertisement read in part:

> As members of the legal profession, we are alarmed by the action of the President in extending the war into Cambodia. We are deeply concerned that the divisions caused by this war endanger our fundamental institutions.
>
> On May 20, 1970, we will cease, to the extent consistent with our professional responsibilities, our usual business and devote our efforts

exclusively toward ending with [*sic*] war in Indochina. We seek . . .
immediate withdrawal from Cambodia, the earliest possible termination of our involvement in Indochina and a return to the rule of law at
home and abroad.[21]

The convocation the night before the trip was attended by six hundred. The speakers included the seventy-nine-year–old retired Chief
Justice, Earl Warren, Senator George McGovern, Plimpton, and Botein. The tone was set by Plimpton, who asserted: "When the President ordered American troops to invade Cambodia, he was acting on
his own, in blithe and unilateral disregard of the Congress. . . . . there
is no record in American history of any such presidential presump-
tion."[22]

As part of his remarks, Botein said at the meeting hall that if the
former presidents of the organization "could see what we're up to
now, they'd be spinning in their frames."[23]

The retired Chief Justice did not mince words. He said that the
war in Indochina had "brought to fever pitch our crisis, already
heightened by racial tensions, crime, poverty, inflation and pollution
of the environment," and that the trip would be "an important step
in bringing our children back to us with the knowledge that we do
care for our country and for them and their future."[24]

Among the later presidents to go on the trip to Washington were
Orville Schell, Adrian DeWind, and Robert McKay. Members of the
delegation spoke to Attorney General John Mitchell, Solicitor General Erwin Griswold, and Under-Secretary of State Elliot Richardson.

While the *Times* advertisement, the May 19th meeting, Plimpton's
activities (he had spent the day prior to the Washington trip organizing a session of the American Law Institute to discuss the spread of
war), and the participation of so many leaders on the Washington trip
left some impression at the time and an increasingly strong impression over time that the Association had sponsored the Washington
trip, it had not. The Association did not go on the record against the
War formally until a meeting eight days later.

The historic meeting of May 28th was one of the most rambunctious in the Association's history. Judge Botein's term as president

had just begun. Presiding over the meeting was an ordeal by fire. Plimpton would speak of the meeting as "a shambles," while Botein called it "the most heated meeting in history."[25]

There were more than one hundred members and a great many non-members in attendance. Non-members were repeatedly asked to leave the hall, and arrangements were made to broadcast the proceedings elsewhere in the House. Nevertheless, some "guests" remained in the room, as did members of the Lawyers Collective, one of whom was permitted to address the meeting for two minutes.

The meeting was marked by lengthy disputes over procedural issues—whether there was a quorum; whether the notice of the meeting contained an adequate statement of the agenda; whether the resolutions were *ultra vires* under the constitution and bylaws of the Association—and by motions to table and queries as to whether those in attendance were in fact members of the Association.

There were four resolutions introduced by Adrian DeWind and endorsed by sixty-five other members under consideration. One was procedural. The other three read:

> RESOLVED, that the Association of the Bar of the City of New York is deeply concerned about the legal basis of the recent decision of the President of the United States to engage United States military forces in Cambodia; calls upon the President of the United States to seek the consent of the Congress of the United States before undertaking any further expansion of the conflict in Southeast Asia; and hereby authorizes and directs the Special Committee on the Lawyer's Role in the Pursuit of Peace to prepare a report concerning the legality (under the Constitution and Laws of the United States and under international law) of the aforesaid decision of the President of the United States and the military engagements resulting therefrom, and to submit such report to the President of the Association not later than June 15, 1970.

> RESOLVED, that The Association of the Bar of the City of New York formally urge the members of the appropriate committees of the Congress of the United States to consider carefully the legal implications of the aforesaid decision of the President of the United States prior to taking action with respect to any additional appropriations for the military services of the United States.

RESOLVED, that The Association of the Bar of the City of New York strongly opposes the extension of the Viet-Namese war into Cambodia and calls for the immediate withdrawal of all United States military forces from that state.[26]

Francis Plimpton presented the case for the antiwar resolutions. Whitney North Seymour, among the most influential members of the Association and a former president, led the opposition.[27] The substantive debate was much more over the *efficacy* of the Association's involvement than over the merits of the resolutions. After four hours, the Association by a vote of 197 to 64 adopted one resolution, an amended and strengthened version of the third resolution, as put forward by Paul Asofsky:

RESOLVED, that The Association of the Bar of the City of New York strongly opposes the continued American involvement in the war in Indochina and strongly urges the immediate withdrawal of all American military forces therefrom.

Just two members of the Association resigned in protest over the antiwar activities. However, a newly formed New York Committee to Support the War, led by Whitney North Seymour and including Orison Marden and Thomas E. Dewey, battled back with newspaper advertisements.

A few days after the May 28th meeting, there was a calmer forum on Cambodia at the House at which Robert McKay, Abram Chayes, and John P. Stevenson (Legal Advisor to the Department of State) participated. So did Assistant Attorney General William H. Rehnquist, who defended the legality of the Administration's position, calling it "precisely the sort of tactical decision traditionally confided to the commander-in-chief in the conduct of armed conflict."[28]

A resolution condemning American involvement in the Indo-China War came before the annual meeting of May 23, 1972. Supported by Plimpton and Eugene Nickerson, among others, it was opposed by Whitney North Seymour, who pointed out that an emotional attack on the war would be harmful to the prestige of the Association, and Arthur Dean, who differed on the substance. The resolution was adopted by a vote of 136 to 66 with two abstentions.[29]

In 1972, after consulting with a special committee that included Ernest A. Gross, Philip C. Jessup, Telford Taylor, Louis Henkin, Wolfgang Friedmann, Adrian DeWind, and Robert MacCrate, President Botein wrote President Nixon, Vice President Agnew, and the Speaker of the House urging creation of a national commission to investigate whether U.S. troops were obeying the laws of war in Indo-China as well as the adequacy of the existing rules as applied to contemporary conflict and weaponry: "Doubts exist concerning the compatibility of certain policies of the United States with the laws of war and the adequacy of governmental processes for assuring compliance with such laws."[30] The proposal was turned down by Nixon by way of a letter from the White House Counsel, John W. Dean, from whom more would be heard by the nation.[31]

One can fairly ask whether the Association's activities opposing the War in Indo-China, especially the Washington trip, made any difference. Botein thought the march "was very important because of the character of the people who went on it," led by Plimpton, an impeccable "Establishment" figure. This was one demonstration where "The marchers were no fringe. They had reasonable haircuts, and they were largely well dressed, with collars and ties and, in many cases, three-piece suits." This was, Botein thought, "very impressive to some congressmen."[32] Schell looked at the trip in organizational terms and called it "one of the best things for the bar that's ever happened. It bridged the generation gap."[33] Plimpton reflected in light verse at the Association's Twelfth Night Party:

> And then it shook you up and snowed ya
> When he said "Invade Cambodia"
>
> Without the least advice congressional,
> That feat belongs in his confessional,
>
> But led of course to that famed train ride—
> Let no one say it was a vain ride,
>
> For think of all the assist ventral
> We gave the ailing old Penn Central,

Postponing for a time, though short,
The embrace of the federal court.[34]

CARSWELL

It is a little easier to assess the impact of the Association's efforts in opposing the nomination of G. Harold Carswell, appointed by Richard Nixon to fill the vacancy on the Supreme Court caused by the resignation of Abe Fortas in 1969. Shortly after Fortas resigned under an ethical cloud, Nixon had appointed Warren Burger Chief Justice, a nomination that aroused little controversy. To the Fortas vacancy Nixon first appointed Clement Haynsworth, Chief Judge of the U.S. Court of Appeals for the Fourth Circuit. Haynsworth was a man of considerable ability who had the misfortune to be appointed to the Supreme Court at the wrong time. Because of the overheated politics of the time, Haynsworth was vulnerable because of a judicial record that demonstrated little enthusiasm for civil rights and less for the rights of labor, as well as because of some comparatively minor ethical problems. Nixon, continuing to play his Southern card, then chose Carswell, a former federal district judge who had been sitting on the U.S. Court of Appeals for the Fifth Circuit for a short time. Carswell was a much less distinguished choice than Haynsworth. Even so, after the bruising Haynsworth struggle, it appeared unlikely that the Senate could muster its strength for another battle with the White House.

That was the situation on February 17, 1970, the day of the Association's centennial convocation. In remarks made that evening Francis Plimpton compared Carswell (and Haynsworth) to Nixon's first Supreme Court nominee, Burger, who was on the podium. "I cannot help expressing the wish," Plimpton said, "that the President of the United States' second and third nominees to the Supreme Court of the United States would have approached, in stature, experience and integrity, his first nominee."[35] At the time, Carswell had not yet been evaluated by the American Bar Association. Plimpton's was one of the first public criticisms of Carswell by a prominent attorney.

Just a few days earlier, Plimpton joined former presidents Sam

Rosenman* and Bethuel Webster, and Bruce Bromley, one of the most prominent members of the New York Bar, in signing a 3,000-word statement critical of Carswell. The statement strongly criticized Carswell's role in incorporating a segregated golf club in Tallahassee:

> The testimony indicates quite clearly that the nominee possesses a mental attitude which would deny to the black citizens of the United States—and to their lawyers, black or white—the privileges and immunities which the Constitution guarantees. It has shown, also, that quite apart from any ideas of white supremacy and ugly racism, that he does not have the legal or mental qualifications essential for service on the Supreme Court, or any high court in the land, including the one where he now sits.[36]

At the suggestion of an aide to Senator Birch Bayh of Indiana, who had emerged as the leader of the opposition to Carswell's confirmation, the statement was not immediately issued, but instead circulated among attorneys and law professors. On March 12th the statement was released at a news conference at the National Press Club attended by Plimpton, Rosenman, and the deans of Yale, Harvard, and the University of Pennsylvania Law Schools. It would give the opposition to Carswell an enormous boost.

The statement, entitled "Judge Carswell does not have the Legal or Mental Qualifications Essential for Service on the Supreme Court," was signed by 133 lawyers and 325 professors from forty-two law schools. Signatories from New York included Robert McKay, Walter Gellhorn, Milton Handler, Herbert Wechsler, Telford Taylor, George N. Lindsay, Cyrus Vance, and Simon Rifkind.[37] The statement cited civil rights cases that Carswell had decided as a district judge against black Americans, cases in which he had been unanimously reversed by appellate courts. Those cases indicated "a closed mind on the subject—a mind impervious to repeated appellate rebuke."[38]

This statement would be referred to frequently in the Senate debates over Carswell. New York Senator Jacob Javits said, for example, "When three former presidents of the Association of the Bar of the

---

*Judge Rosenman would die on June 24, 1973, at the age of seventy-seven.

City of New York, including such traditionalists as Judge Bromley, Francis T. P. Plimpton, and Sam Rosenman, come out against Judge Carswell, it seems to me it is singularly impressive."[39] Senator Clifford Case of New Jersey would say: "We do not get a Bruce Bromley . . . or a Webster . . . or a Judge Rosenman . . . or a Plimpton . . . making statements of this sort lightly. Their consciences were outraged by this appointment."[40] Both Javits and Case were Republicans. Plimpton also persuaded George Ball to present the anti-Carswell case to J. William Fulbright, Democrat of Arkansas, who eventually voted against Carswell.

Traditionally, the Association had never commented on a nominee for the U.S. Supreme Court unless he had come from New York or had practiced in the state, and originally it had decided to follow that precedent in the matter of Carswell. But, after a special meeting called at the request of the Young Lawyers Committee, the Executive Committee changed its mind, because "sufficient unchallenged facts had become part of the public record to establish in the judgment of the Committee that Judge Carswell failed to meet the high standards required for service on the U.S. Supreme Court."[41] The Executive Committee, which included Plimpton, Louis Craco, J. Lee Rankin, Whitman Knapp, and Robert Morgenthau, adopted a resolution urging the Senate to reject the nomination:

> Service on the United States Supreme Court requires that a Justice have exceptional qualifications of integrity, professional distinction, legal learning and proven sensitivity to human and civil rights. In our considered opinion, the public record demonstrates that Judge Carswell lacks these essential qualifications for a Justice of the highest court in the land.[42]

While it was Carswell's racial views that made possible the forging of a coalition similar to that which had rallied against Haynsworth, the opposition of the City Bar was extremely helpful in making viable the second reason to oppose Carswell—his mediocrity. Carswell was defeated by a vote of 51 to 45.

In May 1970, the Executive Committee approved a statement announcing a change in the Association's policy with regard to Supreme

Court nominations. The Association could "express its views con-
-cerning the qualifications of any nominee for the Supreme Court of
the United States, providing that the Executive Committee feels it
has sufficient information to reach an informed decision on the matter." The Association also made recommendations to the American
Bar Association, which had not emerged from the Carswell battle
covered with glory, concerning the procedure it thought the ABA
Committee on the Judiciary should follow in passing on U.S. Supreme Court nominees.[43]

Irrepressible, Plimpton reflected on the experience in rhyme at
the Association's annual Twelfth Night party later in the year:

> Perhaps it wasn't pain's worth
> To worry much about that Haynsworth
>
> But if you really want some scars, well,
> Just think of that High Court with Carswell.
>
> That he's not there's a minor miracle
> For which we chant *Te Deums* lyrical
>
> and venture the mild observation
> 'Twas helped by this Association.[44]

A decade later, Plimpton spoke less lightly about the battle: "Well,
Carswell was just a bad odor, and he was not a very good judge. And
people who were not very good judges should not go on the Supreme
Court."[45]

In 1971, the Association supported the nomination of Lewis F.
Powell, Jr., to the Supreme Court, but was silent about that of William H. Rehnquist.

The battles over the War and Carswell posed difficult questions
about the issues upon which the Association should speak and who
should speak for it. Plimpton himself wrote, "one man's non-partisan
issue is another man's political donnybrook."[46] The Special Committee on the Second Century was asked to address the issue, but could
not devise a bright-line test for determining the kinds of public ques-

tions about which the Association might appropriately speak. The committee was, nevertheless, clear that "in the end the reputation of the Association as a serious force in public questions depends radically upon the preservation of [its] . . . sense of competence."[47]

That 200 members were able to place the imprimatur of a 9,000-member association on one side of a bitterly fought political issue troubled thoughtful members on both sides of the Cambodia issue, as well as the less thoughtful *Daily News* which asked caustically, "Really, isn't it time for the city bar association to change its rules so as to keep the tail from wagging the dog and thereby making the dog look like a jackass?"[48] Botein was concerned that the procedures of his era were "fraught with danger that a small minority can commit the Association publicly to positions that may not reflect the attitudes of a majority of members."[49]

As a result of the tumultuous Cambodia meeting, stringent limitations were placed on what could be done at a stated or other membership meeting. The full text of any resolution to be voted on at a meeting of members would have to be published well in advance, so that all members would be fully informed and could plan to attend should they wish. Furthermore, resolutions could be amended from the floor only if the proposed amendment did not substantially depart from the terms of the original resolution. In addition, in 1975 the bylaws were amended to provide that in matters of "general public interest" a resolution introduced at the members' meeting could be submitted to the entire membership at referendum, should 45 percent of those present at a meeting so desire. Nevertheless, the Executive Committee would increasingly be vested with authority to speak for the Association on many matters.[50]

The president of the Association, however, would not be muzzled. Plimpton, for example, rejected the view that "each president inherits a muzzle with his non-existent mantle," but thought that the president, "making clear that he is standing as an individual, should not hesitate to speak out forcefully on issues of legal significance."[51] Further, the Special Committee on the Second Century emphasized "that the use of the Association's name in forwarding any public cause should be based upon a serious and reasoned consideration of the issues involved in that cause and of the development and presentation of a position in a distinctively professional way."[52] For this, prime reliance would be placed on the committees.

INTERNAL CHANGES

There were important changes in the governance of the Association between 1968 and 1972. In 1970, for the first time in the history of the Association, there was a contested election. Activist, younger members—the "Young Turks"—among them Matthew Mallow, Neal Johnston, Carol Bellamy, and Bob Craft, ran a slate for the Executive Committee: Peter Fleming of Curtis, Mallet-Prevost, Cole & Mosle; Leon Polsky, counsel to the State Narcotics Addiction Control Commission; and John Horan. The slate was defeated by the "Establishment" candidates: Leslie Arps, who received 149 votes, Maurice Rosenberg (148), George P. Kramer (135), and Alfred J. Scotti (129). Horan received 105 votes; Fleming, 98; Polsky, 98.[53]

The next year, however, a slate of three "Young Turks" won: Michael Varet, age 29, of Paul Weiss; Matthew Mallow, age 28, of Marshall Bratter; and Sheilah Avril McLean, age 29, who at the time was at Cravath Swaine & Moore. That year, George Gallantz was the only "Establishment" candidate to win a seat on the Executive Committee.

The effects of the "revolt" were marked. The ambience of the Executive Committee changed dramatically. No longer did its meetings begin in the middle of the afternoon with cocktails and cigars and end at 11. Instead, there would be much briefer business meetings with sandwiches served.

At a meeting on January 5, 1972, in response to efforts of the three Young Turks and with the support of Francis Plimpton, amendments to the constitution and bylaws were adopted by a vote of 172 to 3. These amendments made the Executive Committee the nominating committee for the presidency of the Association, a change that would last only a few years. Additionally, mail ballots would be used in elections, permitting greater participation.[54]

In the future, the nominating committee would deliberately try to make the Executive Committee more diverse and would succeed.[55]

After the election of McLean, the first woman ever to serve on the Executive Committee, there would be a woman in every "class" of four persons elected to the Executive Committee. Youth would also be much better represented on the Executive Committee. African-Americans would regularly be nominated.

There would be other changes in governance. The stated meeting would decline as an important decision-making venue. The office of vice president would be vested with new authority. The influence of the former presidents (sometimes known as the "Former Livings") would be diluted.

The procedure for admission to membership was made simpler and less daunting in 1972. Instead of continuing as a "gate-keeper," the Admissions Committee began to consider how it could play a role in broadening the base of membership. Ultimately, the Admissions Committee was abolished, and the Committee on New Members was created, with increased responsibilities.

Thus, without a doubt, the long-run effect of the "revolt" of 1970 would be a more diversified Association, one more concerned with *pro bono* activities and even more willing to take positions on controversial questions.[56]

Once the "Old Guard" realized that the new political force was not just "making points on the war" but serious about its involvement in the Association, a *modus vivendi* developed—and developed within a year. In some areas where existing committees might have been less than sympathetic, special committees were created to outflank them. Plimpton had already established special committees on consumer affairs and on the environment. Botein received Executive Committee support for special committees on Sex and Law and on criminal justice (the latter chaired by Herbert Brownell).[57] These, in turn, attracted the energies of a different segment of the bar and increased Association involvement in new (and often controversial) issues.

One such issue was consumer protection. Reflecting a generation later about the Consumer Affairs Committee, Evan Davis spoke of it as an "informal, rowdy band of consumer advocates with a few corporate types to keep us honest."[58] That committee would staunchly support class actions and an increase in the powers of the Federal Trade

Commission. In the new ambience the Consumer Affairs Committee was able to carry other committees along.[59] On April 27, 1971, for example, Stephen C. Kass, the chairman of the Special Committee on Consumer Affairs, joined by Sheldon H. Elsen, chairman of the Committee on Federal Legislation, testified before the Consumer Subcommittee of the Senate Commerce Committee supporting federal class action legislation. The Committees on the Federal Courts and Trade Regulation also joined in a report supporting the legislation. (That the Committee on Trade Regulation, traditionally a pro-business committee, went along was the result of Plimpton's appointment of a chairman with some independence from the antitrust defense bar.) Indeed, volume 26 of *The Record* (1971) might well be called the consumer protection volume, with six articles, reports, and bibliographies on that area of the law.[60]

A second was gender equality. The Committee on Sex and Law would cause the reversal of the Association's stand on the Equal Rights Amendment. In November 1970 the Committee on Federal Legislation had opposed ERA, because it believed that the problems ERA was supposed to attack would be dealt with substantially better "by a broad statutory declaration of principle, coupled with specific, carefully drafted legislation directed at specific types of discrimination, and developed by judicial decision." The Committee felt that the Equal Rights Amendment might cause uncertainty and breed litigation, while a statute could be more precise and specific and stand on a sounder legal footing. Conrad Harper dissented from the report.[61]

In 1972 the Committee on Sex and Law, chaired by Orville Schell with Merrell Clark, Jr., Carol Bellamy, and Eleanor Holmes Norton among its members, joined by the Committee on Civil Rights (chaired by Robert Kaufman), urged adoption of the Equal Rights Amendment "as the best means of establishing equality before the law and effecting a comprehensive and constant review of the whole body of legislation which treats men and women differently on the basis of their membership in a sexual class."[62] That became the Association position.

Changes in related matters can be seen during this period. Two years earlier, the Committee on Medicine and Law had been authorized by the Executive Committee to file an action challenging the constitutionality of the New York State abortion statute and supporting its repeal.[63] The first apparent indication of concern about the treatment of gay men and lesbians under the law to appear in *The Record* occurred in June 1972 with the mention of a symposium on "Discrimination Against Homosexuals" moderated by then-Professor Ruth Bader Ginsburg.[64] Ginsburg would serve on the Sex and Law Committee and be frequently consulted before and after her service. In op-ed pieces, she would employ City Bar reports supporting the ERA.[65]

The Association facilitated the efforts of many Wall Street Lawyers to directly give time to assist the poor, while also assisting those public-interest lawyers giving their full professional time. With Legal Aid and the Practising Law Institute, the Association organized a series of practical "how-to-do-it" lectures for the permanent staffs of OEO neighborhood law offices.[66]

Perhaps the best example of the way the Association sought to accommodate the needs of and attract younger lawyers was its relationship with the Council of New York Law Associates. The council had been created in 1969 by associates in the larger law firms to represent their concerns about the distribution of legal services and to increase their *pro bono* work.[67] The Association was supportive, giving the council free space and logistical support, but the relationship was informal and non-institutionalized. The council would become a useful source of volunteer manpower for activities the Association had an interest in, and the council "developed ideas which were helpful to activities undertaken by the Association."[68]

Perhaps the best example of the value of the relationship between the Association and the council is suggested by the work of the Committee on Demonstration Observation. Out of the bloody confrontation of May 8, 1970, between construction workers (some carrying pipes and tools) and peace demonstrators in lower New York came a request from Mayor John Lindsay and Police Commissioner Howard Leary. The May 8th imbroglio had stirred immediate controversy about police action and/or inaction. Lindsay and Leary requested that the Association establish a corps of lawyers to observe and report on police actions at demonstrations. The Association agreed and with the help of the council recruited 150 lawyer-observers. Each of these lawyer-observers went through training programs at the police academy on police methods of crowd control and at the Association on the rights of citizens in demonstrations. The program was based on the belief that if neutral persons of integrity were placed at the scene of demonstrations, not only would events be reported objectively, but there might also be a marked reduction in bodily injuries as well as injuries to property.

The mechanism worked. Observers mingled with demonstrators and police, moved freely across police lines, and inspected procedures at precinct houses. Not a single observer was injured in the first eighteen months of the program. During calendar year 1971, the first year during which the Committee operated, complaints about police activity at demonstrations dropped from 211 to 64. Police misconduct and demonstrator misconduct were not often observed. Most arrests were made without incident. The initial hostility to the observers of both police and demonstrators greatly dissipated. The program was judged a " 'sparkling success.' "[69]

By 1974, the panel had covered 208 demonstrations in three and a half years.[70] Mayor Lindsay credited the group with having "increased public confidence, protected our police from unfounded charges and cooled tempers in some explosive situations."[71]

Thus, the Association's approach to the younger members was, for the most part, inclusive (although there were some bylaw changes to limit their impact). As word spread of changed admissions procedures and greater democratization and as the Association was heard on some of the most burning issues of the time, the City Bar became more attractive to younger lawyers.[72] In the early 1970s, the Association would surpass the New York County Lawyers' Association in the number of new young members.[73] By the end of the 1970s the young lawyers were by far the largest age-group in the Association. If they did not take over the Association, they were participating in many of its activities and as part of its leadership.[74] In 1955 the median age at which members were receiving their first committee assignment was 40. By 1978, it had become 34. Of course, the newer members were not, on the whole, very different in terms of their firms and educational background from the older members, and their views on professional issues differed from the older members more in degree than in direction.[75] Thus, the process was under way by which the Association transformed itself from a patrician legal association to one in which age, gender, and ethnicity would be less important than professional standing.[76] The younger members would after 1971 be absorbed into the Association with remarkably little conflict, political or generational. The Association would continue to broaden its membership and leadership base. The older elite who would guide the Association for the rest of the 1970s—Orville Schell, Cyrus Vance, Adrian DeWind, and Merrell Clark, Jr.—were strong liberals who worked well with the younger, often Democratic, Jewish, and female newcomers, making it easy for the Association to take clear, strong positions on social and professional issues.

NOTES

1. Geoffrey T. Hellman, "Profiles: Period-Piece Fellow," *The New Yorker*, December 4, 1971, p. 103.

2. Interviews with Herbert Brownell, March 9, 1995, and Robert MacCrate, February 23, 1995.

3. Interview with Sheldon Oliensis (see above, chap. 1, note 30).

4. Paul Hoffman, *Lions in the Street: The Story of the Great Wall Street Firms* (New York: Saturday Review Press, 1973), p. 214.

5. Bernard Botein, "Report of the President, 1970–71," *The Record*, 26 (October 1971), 541.

6. Ibid., 514.

7. Francis T. P. Plimpton, "Report of the President, 1969–70," *The Record*, 25 (October 1970), 447, 453.

8. Interview with Merrell E. Clark, Jr., May 3, 1995.

9. Plimpton, "Report of the President, 1969–70" (see above, note 7), 452.

10. *The Opera Companion: A Guide for the Casual Operagoer* (New York: Dodd, Mead, 1961); *Verdi: His Music, Life, and Times* (New York: Dodd, Mead, 1963); *The Companion to Twentieth-Century Opera* (New York: Dodd, Mead, 1979); *Aspects of Verdi* (New York: Dodd, Mead, 1988). See also his *The Red Shirt and the Cross of Savoy: The Story of Italy's Risorgimento, 1748–1841* (New York: Dodd, Mead, 1969).

11. George Martin, "Causes and Conflicts," *The Record*, 25 (April 1970), 225–37.

12. This quotation appeared on the back of the dustjacket of the Houghton, Mifflin edition of *Causes and Conflicts*. See also my review of Martin's book in *Fordham Law Review*, 39 (1970), 169.

13. *The Record*, 25 (March 1970), Supplement No. 3, p. 2.

14. Ibid., pp. 4, 6–7.

15. Ibid., pp. 11–12, 14.

16. Ibid., p. 19.

17. Ibid., p. 24.

18. Interview of Francis T. P. Plimpton by Ed Edwin, April 22, 1981 (unpublished oral history on file with Library of the Association), vol. 2, p. 52. See also Hoffman, *Lions in the Street* (see above, note 4), p. 216.

19. Plimpton, "Report of the President, 1969–70" (see above, note 7), 459.

20. Interview of Francis T. P. Plimpton (see above, note 18), vol. 2, p. 52.

21. Hoffman, *Lions in the Street* (see above, note 4), p. 217. The advertisement appeared in the *New York Law Journal*, May 14, 1970, and *New York Times*, May 17, 1970.

22. "Profiles: Period-Piece Fellow" (see above, note 1), 70.

23. *Women's Wear Daily*, May 21, 1970.

24. *New York Times*, May 20, 1970.

25. Hoffman, *Lions in the Street* (see above note 4), p. 220.

26. Association of the Bar of the City of New York, Minutes of Special Meeting, May 28, 1970, p. 3.

27. Powell, *From Patrician to Professional Elite* (see above, chap. 1, note 2), p. 96.

28. *Baltimore Sun*, June 14, 1970.

29. Association of the Bar of the City of New York, Minutes of the Annual Meeting, May 23, 1972, pp. 2–3.

30. See *The Record*, 27 (January 1972), 1ff.

31. *The Record*, 27 (April 1972), 197–99.

32. "Profiles: Period-Piece Fellow" (see above, note 1), 74.

33. Hoffman, *Lions in the Street* (see above, note 4), p. 220.

34. "Profiles: Period-Piece Fellow" (see above, note 1), 74.

35. Hoffman, *Lions in the Street* (see above, note 4), p. 211.

36. Ibid., pp. 211–12. On the Carswell affair, see Richard Harris, *Decision* (New York: Dutton, 1971).

37. *Albuquerque Journal*, March 13, 1970.

38. *New York Times*, March 13, 1970.

39. "Profiles: Period-Piece Fellow" (see above, note 1), 66.

40. Ibid.

41. Plimpton, "Report of the President, 1969–70" (see above, note 7), 458. See also Association of the Bar of the City of New York, Minutes of Annual Meeting of May 26, 1970, p. 5.

42. *New York Law Journal*, March 31, 1970; Kittaning, Pa. *Leader-Times*, March 31, 1970.

43. Association of the Bar of the City of New York, Minutes of the Annual Meeting, May 26, 1970, p. 7.

44. *The Record*, 26 (February 1971), 107, 109.

45. Interview of Francis T. P. Plimpton (see above, note 18), vol. 2, pp. 50–51.

46. Plimpton, "Report of the President, 1969–70" (see above, note 7), 461.

47. Special Committee on the Second Century, "The Decision-Making Structure of the Association" (see above, chap. 1, note 34), 98, 101.

48. New York *Daily News*, May 30, 1970.

49. Bernard Botein, "Report of the President, 1971–72," *The Record*, 27 (October 1972), 457, 458.

50. Powell, *From Patrician to Professional Elite* (see above, chap. 1, note 2), pp. 105–107.

51. Plimpton, "Report of the President, 1969–70" (see above, note 7), 460–61.

52. Special Committee on the Second Century. "Decision-Making Structure of the Association" (see above, note 47).

53. Association of the Bar of the City of New York, Minutes of Special Meeting, May 28, 1970, p. 13.

54. *The Record*, 27 (January 1972), 3–6 (Special Meeting Minutes).

55. Powell, *From Patrician to Professional Elite* (see above, chap. 1, note 2), p. 104.

56. Interviews with Michael A. Cardozo and George G. Gallantz (see above, chap. 1, note 3); Evan Davis (see above, chap. 1, note 30); Robert M. Kaufman, February 3, 1995; William Hellerstein, February 24, 1995; Archibald Murray, March 2, 1995. See also Powell, *From Patrician to Professional Elite* (see above, chap. 1, note 2), pp. 46, 62, 68, 105, 111.

57. Powell, *From Patrician to Professional Elite* (see above, chap. 1, note 2), p. 117; Botein, "Report of the President, 1970–71" (see above, note 5), 505–506.

58. Interview with Evan Davis (see above, chap. 1, note 30).

59. Powell, *From Patrician to Professional Elite* (see above, chap. 1, note 2), p. 120.

60. *The Record*, 26 (October 1971), 421–23, and "Proposed Federal Legislation to Protect Consumers, Including Consumer Class Actions," ibid., 601ff. See also Powell, *From Patrician to Professional Elite* (see above, chap. 1, note 2), pp. 135, 126, 127; interview with Harvey Goldschmid, March 3, 1995.

61. Committee on Federal Legislation, "Amending the Constitution to Prohibit State Discrimination Based on Sex," *The Record*, 26 (January 1971), 77–78.

62. Botein, "Report of the President, 1971–72" (see above, note 49), 465–66.

63. Plimpton, "Report of the President, 1969–70" (see above, note 7), 481.

64. *The Record*, 27 (June 1972), 365–66.

65. Interview with Merrell Clark (see above, note 8). See Ruth Bader Ginsburg, "The Fear of the Equal Rights Amendment," *Washington Post*, April 17, 1995.

66. Francis T. P. Plimpton, "The President's Letter," *The Record*, 24 (February 1969), 74. The Young Lawyers Committee published a list of New York volunteer organizations rendering Legal Assistance to the Poor: "New York Volunteer Organizations Rendering Legal Assistance to the Poor," *The Record*, 24 (October 1969), 458ff., which was regularly updated. See *The Record*, 25 (May 1970), 323–34 and 27 (February 1972), 86–97.

67. Powell, *From Patrician to Professional Elite* (see above, chap 1, note 2), pp. 61, 101–102. See esp. Neil Johnson, "The Council of New York Law Associates," *The Record*, 25 (May 1971), 312ff.

68. Special Committee on the Second Century, "Relationship of the Association to the Community," *The Record*, 29 (January 1974), 72–73.

69. *New York Times*, May 6, 1972; Committee on Demonstration Observations, "Report," *The Record*, 27 (October 1972), Supplement, p. 26.

70. *The Record*, 29 (February 1974), 129.

71. Botein, "Report of the President, 1971–72" (see above, note 49), 461; *Cincinnati Post and Times Star*, December 16, 1970.

72. Powell, *From Patrician to Professional Elite* (see above, chap. 1, note 2), pp. 92, 102, 111.

73. Ibid., pp. 62, 50; interviews with Archibald Murray (see above, note 56), and George G. Gallantz (see above, chap. 1, note 3).

74. Powell, *From Patrician to Professional Elite* (see above, chap. 1, note 2), p. 61.

75. Ibid., pp. 137, 240.

76. Ibid., pp. xxvi, xxi, 228.

3

"The People of the United States Need a Lawyer": The Association of the Bar, 1972–76

DURING THE PERIOD FROM 1972 to 1976, the most celebrated positions taken by the Association involved Watergate. In addition, during these years, long-sought-after goals in *state* judicial selection and lawyer discipline were at least partially achieved, while a number of other important professional matters occupied the Association in the mid-1970s, most notably lawyer advertising and discipline. Under two liberal and able presidents, the turmoil of the preceding years receded, and membership increased and continued to be more and more diverse.

THE PRESIDENTS

The election of Orville Schell as president of the Association in 1972 signaled that the significant changes which had occurred during the Plimpton–Botein presidencies would continue. Schell was one of the leading opponents of the Vietnam War within the Association and had chaired the Committee on Sex and Law. The "young Turks" found Schell "*simpatico.*"[1]

At the time of his election, Orville Schell was sixty-six years old. He came from a family that had lived in the United States since the eighteenth century. But while his ancestors had lived in Pennsylvania Dutch country, Schell grew up in New Rochelle, New York, where his father practiced medicine. Schell attended Lawrenceville, Yale College, and the Harvard Law School. He practiced at Hughes Hubbard & Reed, where he had specialized in litigation, corporate law, and international finance, and handled many mergers for his major client, Merck & Co. Besides his involvement with the Association, which began in 1939, Schell also was director or officer of a great many community activities, including the Union Settlement of Harlem, where he was president. Five feet eight inches and 162 pounds, Schell was always seen in grey suits, "looking as if he had stepped out of a Louis Auchincloss novel." He was not, though, a typical man in a "gray flannel suit," but rather a deeply committed liberal. The writer Jonathan Schell was a son from his first marriage. At the time Orville Schell became president of the City Bar, he had a child of three and one of ten months by his second marriage.[2]

Cyrus Vance, Schell's successor, like William Evarts, Samuel Tilden, Charles Evans Hughes, and Elihu Root, was a leader of the Association who served the United States in high office as an independent and honorable public servant. Vance was born in Clarksburg, West Virginia, on March 27, 1917. His father died when he was a child. Vance's *de facto* guardian, his cousin John W. Davis, one of the great American lawyers of the century (and a former president of the Association), imbued him with a sense of the importance of public service and the lawyer's obligation to provide equal justice for all.[3]

Vance attended Yale College and Yale Law School, then served on destroyers in the Atlantic and Pacific during the Second World War. He joined Simpson Thacher & Bartlett in 1947, beginning, as he described it, "by carrying Whitney North Seymour's briefcase." From 1957 to 1960, when serving as Special Counsel to the Subcommittee of the Senate Armed Services Committee and counsel to the Special Subcommittee on Space and Aeronautics, Vance worked closely with Lyndon Johnson.

Under President John F. Kennedy, Vance served as General Counsel to Secretary of Defense Robert McNamara, as Secretary of the Army and as Deputy Secretary of Defense. When Lyndon Johnson became President, Vance served as his Special Representative and troubleshooter in a series of difficult crises—supervising the U.S. military effort to prevent a Communist takeover in the Dominican Republic, mediating the Cyprus conflict, directing the federal military force in Detroit during the racial riots, conducting intensive negotiations with President Park and others in Korea after the seizure of the *Pueblo* and raid on the Blue House by the North Koreans, and advising Mayor Walter Washington of the nation's capital after the riots that followed Martin Luther King's assassination. Finally, Johnson appointed Vance and Averell Harriman peace negotiators with North Vietnam (1968–69).

Vance returned to New York with the change in administration in 1969 and again became active in the Association of the Bar. Previously, he had served on the Committee on Criminal Courts (1950–53), Municipal Affairs (1956–59), and as a member of the Executive Committee (1968–72). He would also serve as a member of the Committee on International Arms Control and Security Affairs (1972–74) and as chair of the Special Committee on the Second Century (1972–74). He also was a member of the Commission to Investigate Police Corruption in New York City ("Knapp Commission") (1970–72).

While consideration of Vance's service as Secretary of State from 1977 to 1980 goes beyond the scope of this study, it is fair to say that he was a steady, patient negotiator who won respect from foreign leaders for his directness and honesty as diplomatic hocus-pocus and self-promotion were antithetical to him. Moving "easily and gracefully through the corridors of power," he resigned the office in 1980 on principle when President Jimmy Carter went ahead with the mission to rescue the hostages in Iran.[4]

THE ASSOCIATION AND WATERGATE

The Watergate scandal provoked the most dramatic events in the life of the Association between 1972 and 1976. In the Plimpton–Botein years, the Association had strongly opposed the Nixon Administration over Cambodia and Carswell. There also had been sharp differences over reporters' privilege legislation, executive privilege, and the proper way to amend the Voting Rights Act.[5] Further, when the President called upon the organized bar in May 1970 to help him get his organized crime legislation through the House (legislation which already had passed the Senate by a vote of 73 to 1), Sheldon Elsen and Robert J. Geniesse of the Committee on Federal Legislation testified against the bill as containing the "seeds of official repression" and presented the Congress with a fifty-three–page committee report opposing the bill. Their opposition was widely publicized.[6] Against this background, it was no surprise that the leaders of the Association of the Bar would speak out strongly against what they saw as a profound challenge to the rule of law.

After James McCord's letter, which stated that the Watergate burglars had been paid hush money, was read in open court by Judge John J. Sirica on March 23, 1973, the Watergate cover-up began to unravel. The President's counsel, John W. Dean, began plea negotiations, and it became increasingly clear that two of the most trusted aides to the President, H. R. Haldeman and John Ehrlichman, were involved in the scandal, as was former Attorney General John Mitchell. The current Attorney General, Richard Kleindienst, also appeared to be tainted. After the President accepted the resignations of Kleindienst, Haldeman, and Ehrlichman with high praise and fired Dean, Orville Schell, then Association president, wrote an open letter to Nixon calling for appointment of a completely independent prosecutor, and the Association supplied Congress with a draft bill![7] Schell also wrote an "op-ed" piece for *The New York Times* which stressed that the investigation of Watergate had been marked by conflicts of interest at the highest levels:

> For too long the reins of [the] Watergate investigation have been held in the hands of the very people being investigated. The people of the United States have a right [to] demand that the investigation immediately be put into the hands of an independent, able special counsel who will act for the people in whom they can have full confidence and who will have full authority to look down every dark alley of the whole affair.[8]

"Like it or not," the President may be involved, Schell said, and if so, "the President and his administration must be investigated, [and that] cannot be done by his own lawyer." "The people of the United States," Schell concluded, "need a lawyer."[9]

Rarely in American history has an independent bar (or a concerned electorate) been more important than during that weekend in October 1973 when the "Saturday Night Massacre" occurred. Special Prosecutor Archibald Cox had finally been discharged by Acting Attorney General Robert Bork after Attorney General Elliot Richardson and Deputy Attorney General William Ruckelshaus had resigned rather than do so. The office of the Special Prosecutor had been sealed by the FBI. Schell immediately spoke out. "The President's disgraceful and cynical game plan of this weekend," he said, "does not return us to a government under law." The bottom line "is that Nixon is setting himself as the sole judge of what goes on in this country, and that is contrary to all our principles of separation of powers and certainly it is a devastating blow to the rule of law." By this, the President had "lost all moral standing to be the leader of our country." "Speaking personally," Schell added, "and not as President [of the Association], I'm for impeachment."[10]

On October 24, four days after the "Massacre," the Association announced that Cox, the fired Special Prosecutor, had accepted an invitation to speak on November 12. Unsuccessful efforts were made to have the President's personal lawyer, Charles Alan Wright, speak on the same program.

The evening Cox spoke—his first speech after the firing—was one of the great evenings in the history of the Association. There was a completely packed house. The Harvard patrician, wearing his characteristic bow tie, received a standing ovation. Cox spoke of the extraordinary public outcry that had followed his firing, the "fire storm" that had caused Nixon to reverse his position and turn over subpoenaed tape recordings, as having its source in the "longing of countless simple, direct and moral people for a greater measure of candor, simplicity and rectitude in the conduct of government." As he looked back over the events, Cox said that "surely those of us who are dedicated to constitutionalism and the rule of law can take heart in the public outcry and the resulting Presidential turnabout." "For those events," he concluded, "demonstrate better than any other occurrence within memory the extent of this country's dedication to the principle that ours is a government of laws and not of men—and of the people's determination and ability to insist that the highest officials shall meet their obligations under the law as fully and faithfully as other members of the public."[11]

At its November 1973 meeting the Association adopted the following resolution:

RESOLVED, that the Association of the Bar of the City of New York approves and supports the actions taken by the Judiciary Committee of the House of Representatives to investigate whether or not impeachment proceedings should be instituted against the President of the United States. Because of the public importance of this issue, we urge that the committee report its conclusions at the earliest practicable time.[12]

During the months impeachment was under consideration by the House of Representatives, the Committee on Federal Legislation, chaired by Martin F. Richman, made an important contribution to public education with publication of *The Law of Impeachment*. The booklet was essentially a straightforward guide to the impeachment process. On the central legal issue, the authors of the booklet took the position that a President may be impeached for acts which *are not* violations of the ordinary criminal law and also for acts which "undermine the integrity of government," including conduct "amounting to a gross breach of trust." The authors stated, however, that the framers of the Constitution had rejected "an open-ended purely political reach for the impeachment power." One hundred thousand copies of the booklet were published in the first printing.[13] The booklet was widely discussed and quoted. The *New York Law Journal* published the report in a two-part article. *Time* wrote an essay based on it. Newspapers from *The New York Times* to the *Stillwater* [Maine] *Gazette* wrote editorials using it. Other newspapers from all over the country—newspapers in Allentown, New Orleans, Concord, and Memphis, just to mention some—used the booklet to help educate the citizenry.[14]

After President Gerald Ford's pardon of Nixon, the Executive Committee authorized the Association's president to release the following statement:

Government is founded on the principle of equal justice for all. Lawyers have a special commitment to that principle. Ordinarily the power to pardon has been exercised only if there has been a finding of guilt and after a full, fair and open trial. The power to pardon is a sacred trust to be used only in the rare circumstance that full justice requires that it be tempered by mercy. On the basis of the facts now available, the Association believes that President Ford acted prematurely and unwisely in issuing an unconditional pardon to Richard M. Nixon.

Any further use of that power in connection with the Watergate Affair at this time, whatever its motive, would have the effect of keeping hidden the facts which justice and, therefore, the welfare of the nation demand be revealed. . . .[15]

As early as 1973, the Grievance Committee of the Association had been gathering evidence related to the lawyers involved in the Watergate scandals. An *ad hoc* national committee, the Special Committee to Coordinate Watergate Discipline, formed under the auspices of the National Organization of Bar Counsel, linked the grievance committees throughout the nation in investigating the misconduct of several dozen lawyers. However, information that the Association's Grievance Committee was "quietly investigating allegations of professional misconduct" by Nixon and John Mitchell was leaked to the press in April 1974 and widely publicized. (Nixon had become a member of the New York Bar in the 1960s when he joined John Mitchell's firm, a firm renamed Nixon Mudge Rose Guthrie Alexander & Mitchell.[16])

After Nixon resigned as President and was pardoned, he was successful in resigning from the California bar so as to avoid disbarment. He tried the same thing in New York, but did not succeed. The Grievance Committee proceeded to investigate him, employing Arthur Liman as special counsel. "Very conscious about fairness to the President," the committee moved carefully.[17] Eventually, the Grievance Committee petitioned the Appellate Division, First Department to take action against Nixon. There were five allegations of misconduct, including obstruction of the FBI inquiry into the Watergate burglary, improper approval of the payment of hush money to the Watergate burglars, and improper obstruction of the investigation of the burglary of Daniel Ellsburg's psychiatrist. A copy of the petition was sent to Nixon's attorney, who informed the Association that Nixon would not accept service. The Association then sought to achieve service through the office of the sheriff of Orange County, California, but Nixon, through an aide, refused to accept the papers. Ultimately, he was served by mail. Nixon never responded personally; nor did he appear by counsel or file papers in the matter.

The Appellate Division held that Nixon was not entitled to resign without admitting guilt. It then disbarred him, holding that each allegation was substantiated by documentary evidence (and that Nixon's failure to answer or appear would be construed as admissions). The Court held:

> The gravamen of respondent's misconduct is obstruction of the due administration of justice, a most serious offense, but one which is rendered even more grievous by the fact that in this instance the perpetrator is an attorney and was at the time of the conduct in question the holder of the highest public office of this country and in a position of public trust.[18]

Nixon was struck from the roll of attorneys and counselors at law, effective August 9, 1976. This was the first time any official body had found Nixon guilty of Watergate-related charges.[19] John Mitchell was also disbarred after his conviction for involvement in the Watergate coverup.[20]

Although they did not arouse the interest of the Nixon disbarment, two other grievance matters during this period are worthy of mention. One involved the radical lawyer William Kunstler, who had been convicted of contempt of court for his conduct during the trial of the Chicago 7 in 1969–70. During a tough campaign for U.S. Senator from New York in 1970, James Buckley called for Kunstler's disbarment in campaign speeches and, then, in a blitz of publicity, personally filed his complaint with the Grievance Committee.[21]

Although the Grievance Committee did not act when under that kind of political pressure, it did act in 1974 *before* Kunstler had exhausted his appeals in the contempt case, bringing disciplinary charges against him. Unanimously disagreeing with the Grievance Committee, the Executive Committee of the Association held that the Grievance Committee had improperly disregarded a long-standing policy by acting before all appeals had been exhausted. The charges were then withdrawn by the Grievance Committee under instruction from the Appellate Division.[22]

Additionally, in 1971, Martin Erdmann, senior Legal Aid attorney, was quoted in a *Life* Magazine article vividly criticizing New York

courts. Erdmann said: "There are so few trial judges who just judge
. . . who rule on questions of law, and leave guilt or innocence to the
jury. And Appellate Division judges aren't any better. They're the
whores who become madams."[23] The Appellate Division, First Department, not amused, requested that the Grievance Committee investigate, but the committee would not be the court's catspaw,
refusing to initiate action. The First Department itself then acted
and found Erdmann "guilty of official misconduct" by "intemperate,
vulgar and insulting remarks."

Erdmann was not successful in blocking the proceedings in the
Appellate Division, although his case went all the way to the U.S.
Supreme Court. He did, however, finally win on the merits, when
the New York State Court of Appeals reversed the Appellate Division
by a vote of 5 to 2. The State's highest court held that "isolated instances of disrespect for the law, judges and courts expressed by
vulgar and insulting words and other incivility, uttered, written or
committed outside the precincts of a court are not subject to professional discipline." A few years later, Erdmann was named attorney-
in-charge of Legal Aid's Criminal Defense Division.[24]

JUDICIAL SELECTION, DISCIPLINE, AND ADMINISTRATION

For generations the Association had largely been unsuccessful in
pressing its agenda of: (1) altering the method of judicial selection in
New York State from elective to appointive; (2) then, in the appointing process, deemphasizing politics and emphasizing quality by limiting the governor to selection from a short list of three to five names
provided to him by a nonpartisan and truly representative judicial
selection commission; (3) providing for an effective system for review
of every judge eligible for reappointment (or reelection); (4) providing effective procedures for removal of judges who were derelict in
their duties. During the 1970s progress was made on that agenda in
both the state and the municipal courts (the latter to be discussed in
the next chapter).

After years of inertia, significant progress was made during the
Schell–Vance years. The most important development was the adop-

tion of a state constitutional amendment, followed by passage of a statute providing for gubernatorial appointment of Court of Appeals judges from a short list supplied by a nominating commission. That such progress was made was the result of both increased public concern about removing courts from politics, which was one part of the fallout from the Watergate scandals, and the legacy of several contested elections for the New York Court of Appeals.

Traditionally, when there was a vacancy in the position of Chief Judge of the New York Court of Appeals, the Republican and Democratic parties jointly nominated the senior associate judge for elevation, regardless of his or her party. That system broke down in 1973 when the parties came to fill the vacancy left by the retirement of Chief Judge Stanley Fuld, because the senior associate judge indicated he did not want the job. The Republican Party then nominated the second most senior associate judge, Charles O. Breitel. A fourway race for the Democratic nomination developed. Jack B. Weinstein, United States District Judge for the Eastern District of New York—former Fuld law clerk, Columbia Law professor, and author of the major treatise on New York practice—ran for the Chief Judgeship, arguing quite plausibly that elevation by seniority was not likely to result in the selection of a judge with the administrative abilities that ought to be possessed by the head of the state court system.[25] Weinstein and Breitel were rated "approved and highly qualified" by the Association. Of Weinstein's three opponents, Appellate Division Judge Francis T. Murphy was rated "qualified," while State Supreme Court Justice Irwin R. Brownstein and Jacob B. Fuchsberg, a very able negligence attorney, were rated "not approved." Fuchsberg beat Weinstein in the primary by fewer than 1,000 votes of 750,000 cast. Breitel won the general election.

The following year the seats of three judges of the Court of Appeals were filled in a contested election marked by television advertising. A window of opportunity for reform opened as a result of widespread dissatisfaction with the spectacle of contested elections for the state's highest court. The window opened wider with the election of Hugh Carey as governor in 1974. Cyrus Vance, president of the Association, was named to head Carey's task force on the courts. The members of that task force included Ruth Bader Ginsburg, Mario Cuomo, and

Victor Kovner. Following the recommendations of the task force, Governor Carey in February 1975 issued an executive order creating judicial nominating panels for the Court of Appeals and the Appellate Division.[26] That year, the efforts of the Committee for Modern Courts, the League of Women Voters, the Association, and the governor and his counsel (Judah Gribetz) led the state legislature to propose amendments to the state constitution. One proposed amendment provided for appointment by the governor of Court of Appeals judges from a list of lawyers recommended by a nonpartisan Commission on Judicial Nomination to consist of twelve members— four appointed by the governor, four by the Chief Judge of the Court of Appeals, and four by the leaders of the legislature.

A second amendment proposed by the legislature in 1975 provided for a permanent Commission on Judicial Conduct to have the authority subject to review by the Court of Appeals to remove, censure, or admonish unworthy judges or judges with mental or physical disabilities. The third amendment of 1975 provided for centralized administration of the state courts under the Chief Judge.[27] The amendments went before the voters in November 1977 and passed. Although ratification of the amendments was a huge step forward, the legislature had not satisfied two other long-term goals of the Association—the end of popular election of state lower court judges and unification of the state trial courts.

In 1978 Carey signed into law a bill implementing the three court-reform amendments. The Committee on State Courts of Superior Jurisdiction was unhappy about the number of names (seven) the Judicial Nomination Commission was authorized to submit to the governor for the office of Chief Judge. The committee also disapproved several aspects of the implementation of the Commission on Judicial Conduct.[28]

When Mario Cuomo was elected governor in 1982, a breach seemed to be opening between the governor and the Association when the names put forward by the Judicial Nominating Commission for a Court of Appeals judgeship were all white males. Cuomo threatened not to appoint anyone. The breach was headed off when Louis Craco, then Association president, who was eager to preserve a process vastly better than election, chose to intervene in a nonpublic way to try to find a workable solution. Craco hosted a small dinner in the Tweed Room for the governor and some members of the Association. After a long discussion, the governor agreed to fill the existing vacancy with one of the persons put forward by the commission, with the understanding that in the future the commission would reach out for a more diverse group. One of the fruits of that compromise was the appointment of Judith Kaye to the Court of Appeals several years later.[29]

Two other controversial matters that occurred during the Schell–Vance period ought to be mentioned. In 1974–75, the Association waged its first campaign since the early 1960s to keep a nominee to the lower federal courts off the bench. That was Thomas J. Meskill, who had been nominated by Richard Nixon (on his last day in office), at the behest of Senator Lowell Weicker, to the U.S. Court of Appeals for the Second Circuit. Meskill had been a mayor, two-term U.S. congressman, and governor of Connecticut. The Association of the Bar and the American Bar Association opposed Meskill because he had little practical experience as an attorney and no record of legal scholarship. Some critics complained that he was lacking in judicial temperament and linked him to political scandals. While Meskill's nomination was initially blocked by the Senate Judiciary Committee, it was resubmitted by Gerald Ford. Ultimately, the Judiciary Committee approved the nomination by an 8-to-6 vote and the Senate by 54 to 36. Meskill surprised his critics by achieving a judicial career of distinction.[30]

Secondly, the Association was highly critical of the transfer or, as some called it, "banishment," of Judge Bruce Wright from the Criminal to the Civil Court. Wright, an African-American judge, under sharp attack from the Police Benevolent Association and the *Daily News* for releasing defendants on no or low bail, was called by his critics "Turn-'em-loose Bruce." The ultimate responsibility for the transfer lay with Chief Judge Breitel. In its thirty-page report the Committee on Criminal Courts, Law and Procedure concluded:

> In view of the unwarranted, unique and extensive public criticism of Judge Wright, particularly as to his bail decisions, an unexplained transfer effected during the period of such criticism gave the appear-

ance of an encroachment on the independence of the judiciary, and, therefore, constituted an error in judgment by those who made the transfer, which can only be corrected by the immediate return of Judge Wright to the Criminal Court.[31]

The report also stated that Wright's handling of bail in one of his most notorious cases, that of Joseph Guttola, had been warranted and noted that Guttola's conviction had been upheld by only 4 to 3 in the Court of Appeals, with the three dissenters arguing that the wrong man had been convicted. Angered by the report, Civil Court Judge Charles S. Whitman resigned from the Association.[32]

PROFESSIONAL DEVELOPMENTS

The Association of the Bar of the City of New York has prided itself on not being a trade association. Its emblematic concerns have been broad questions of public policy. Nevertheless, there have always been some important aspects of the Association's activities which have dealt directly with the profession. The Committee on Grievances and the Committee on Professional and Judicial Ethics have been two of the most prominent examples. During the 1970s, there were professional matters of considerable significance which occupied the Association.

The 1970s were a time of major changes in the practice of law. There was an extraordinary increase in the number of law students, in the total number of attorneys, in the number of female law students and attorneys, in the number of attorneys who were employees rather than independent practitioners, and in the income of attorneys. Seventeen new law schools were approved by the ABA between 1968 and 1978. During the 1970s, attorneys were increasing eight times as fast as the population. In the 1970s the percentage of female law students increased to 35 percent. The number of women practicing law increased 250 percent. The size of the large law firms increased greatly during the 1970s and so did the number of corporate counsel, civil servants, prosecutors, and public defenders. The number of legal clinics grew enormously. The aggregate income of attorneys increased from $6 billion (1967) to $16 billion (1972), $19 billion (1977), and $34 billion (1982).[33]

The certification of legal specialists, the problem of civility in court, and lawyer advertising were among the major issues facing the profession in the 1970s. The first two are considered here; the third, in the next chapter.

The broad problem of whether lawyers should be certified in specialized areas emerged most notably in the debate over the certification of trial advocates in federal district court. Chief Justice Warren Burger, who while titular head of the profession often acted as its gadfly, raising questions about litigiousness and low ethical standards, was the most prominent advocate of special standards for those who tried cases in federal district courts. The Association was not an enthusiastic supporter.

New York City was an important venue for the controversy. Burger had speculated upon the "possible causes of the inadequate courtroom performance of far too many American lawyers" and proposed the certification of trial advocates in his 1973 Sonnett Lecture at Fordham Law School. In an address before the New York County Lawyers' Association, Chief Judge Irving R. Kaufman of the United States Court of Appeals for the Second Circuit raised concerns similar to Burger's and then appointed a Committee on Qualifications to practice before the United States Courts in the Second Circuit. The committee was chaired by Robert L. Clare, Jr., of Shearman & Sterling.

The Clare Committee recommended that before a lawyer could be admitted to practice before the courts of the circuit, he or she would have to successfully complete courses in five subject areas. The committee also recommended that candidates for admission to the trial bar of the Second Circuit be required essentially either to have participated in the preparation of four trials or to have observed six. These proposals were accepted in principle by the Judicial Council of the Second Circuit, the Second Circuit Court of Appeals, and the Northern District of New York.

In November 1974 the Committee on Federal Courts of the Association, chaired by Bernard W. Nussbaum (with Joseph McLaughlin, Standish F. Medina, Jr., Burt Neuborne, and Otto G. Obermeier among the members), opposed the adoption of additional requirements for admission to the district courts of the circuit.[34] President Vance appointed a Special Committee on Professional Education and Admissions not only to look into the issue of the competence of the federal bar but also to consider such issues as mandated continuing legal education, bar exams, and the character and fitness process. He expressed the hope that in the interim the federal courts in the Circuit would defer action on the trial advocacy matter, because "[e]fforts to improve the competence of the profession and the rights of those seeking admission to the profession are subjects which peculiarly require a wide consensus before any changes can become effective, even though change is mandated by court rule or otherwise."[35]

The Special Committee on Professional Education and Admissions was chaired by Marvin E. Frankel, then a judge of the Southern District and a formidable man with a pen. Among the other members of the committee were Geoffrey Hazard, Archibald Murray, Judge Sidney Asch, and Louis Craco. On November 20, 1975, the Special Committee opposed the new Second Circuit rules in a joint report with the Committee on Federal Courts. The joint committee thought that the courts "may well have prescribed the wrong medicine for the wrong disease."[36] They doubted that whatever incompetency existed was the result of lack of familiarity with the rules of evidence or procedure or was that of younger, less experienced lawyers. Rather, the joint committee thought the problem lay more "in lack of preparation and failure to take the time required thoroughly to understand cases." The committee expressed its concern that the new standards might decrease access to the federal courts, limit course selection in law school, and itself be a deterrent to meaningful reform. The joint committee then made thirteen recommendations for actions to be undertaken by the courts or the law schools running the gamut from expanding training for advocacy both before and after graduation from law school to the creation of an agency to monitor the competence of counsel. The opponents of the standards won the battle in New York City, for both the Southern and Eastern Districts of New York rejected the rules.

One response from the Association to the controversy was a program of twenty-one lectures and discussions held at the House dealing with the trial of civil and criminal matters in federal court. The distinguished faculty included Rudolph Giuliani, Erwin Griswold, Louis Nizer, Arthur Liman, Irving Younger, Orren Judd, and Margaret Berger.[37]

One of the most important contributions of the Association to professional matters during this period was publication of *Disorder in the Court*, the report of the Special Committee on Courtroom Conduct. In the wake of two highly "political trials"—the Chicago 7 (1969–70) and the New York trial of the Panther 21 (1970–71)—which had been marked by rambunctious defendants and obstructionist attorneys, Chief Justice Burger among others expressed serious concerns about growing incivility in court. President Plimpton had formed a special committee to inquire into the problem of uncivil and ill-mannered lawyers. Chaired by Burke Marshall, former Assistant Attorney General for Civil Rights, the committee included such members as Cyrus Vance, Robert Kaufman, Robert McKay, George N. Lindsay, Jr., Bruce Bromley, and Bethuel Webster.[38]

At the core of *Disorder in the Court* were the results of a comprehensive national survey of trial judges, prosecutors, and other leaders of the bar. The principal finding was that the incidence of courtroom disruptions was "very, very small" and was not growing. According to 1,602 trial judges surveyed, there were only twenty-one instances of courtroom disruptions with political overtones. Out of 630,000 trials throughout the nation in the preceding few years, only 112 outbursts of any kind of recent years were reported from the judges' entire experience.[39] As Burke Marshall stated in the preface:

> If there is an unexpressed underlying message in this report I think it is that at the time Mr. Plimpton appointed our committee, the bar as a whole misconstrued both publicly and in its private councils, the dimensions and causes of courtroom disorders. In speeches, reports, panels, judicial conferences, and other forums, the law professors acted at that time as if the courts of this country had suddenly been taken over by an organized group of radical lawyers interested only in destroying the system that was protecting their clients.[40]

THE WORK OF THE COMMITTEES

By far the greatest amount of significant work of The Association of the Bar of the City of New York is done by its committees. In this study, it is possible to offer only a few examples of important committee work between 1972 and 1976. While the Committee on Federal Legislation has often dealt with subjects of broad public interest, rarely has it dealt with as many highly charged issues in so short a time as it did between 1972 and 1976, when it was chaired, first by Martin F. Richman and then by John D. Feerick. In the spring of 1973, less than a year after the Supreme Court refused to find in the First Amendment a constitutional privilege for reporters not to reveal their sources,[41] the committee endorsed legislation providing for a qualified journalists' privilege. The committee believed such federal legislation warranted under the Constitution and would advance fundamental values without hampering unduly the legitimate interests of law enforcement.[42] The committee provided the Congress with "the first carefully reasoned legal digest of journalists' privilege legislation."[43]

During the Schell/Vance period, the Committee on Federal Legislation counseled against passage of the School Prayer Amendment,[44] supported legislation permitting congressional review and nullification of executive impoundments,[45] and very strongly endorsed gun control legislation. As to the latter, the committee report stated: "The Committee does not find any substantial justification for the continued widespread public possession of handguns, and, accordingly, we strongly endorse the legislative proposals calling for a prohibition on the manufacture, importation, sale, and private possession of handguns."[46]

During these years the Committee on Sex and Law and the Civil Rights Committee dealt for the first time with proposed legislation to prevent discrimination against gay men and lesbians (see p. 163), while the former committee also considered the proposed Equal Rights Amendment (p. 38). The Committee on Civil Rights urged federal legislation to prohibit all military surveillance of civilian political activity and governmental use of tax returns,[47] while opposing the Nixon Administration's bill making renewal of broadcast licenses easier by circumscribing the public's right to be heard and reducing the scope of judicial review.[48] The Committee on Civil Rights and the Committee on International Human Rights sought to tighten control by Congress over the CIA.[49] Endorsement by the Committee on Civil Rights of the restricted use of quotas and affirmative action in employment and higher education "as an interim step, limited in time and scope, for the purpose of achieving a corrective balance," drew considerable criticism.[50]

Among the other significant reports of this period was the recommendation made by the Committee on Criminal Courts, Law and Procedure favoring repeal of corroboration requirements in prosecutions for forcible rape and other forcible sex offenses.[51]

OTHER ACTIVITIES

The Association house is always alive with lectures. The oldest and most prestigious is the annual Benjamin N. Cardozo lecture. Not long after Chief Judge Irving Kaufman delivered the Thirty-Fourth Annual Benjamin N. Cardozo Lecture on "Chilling Judicial Independence,"[52] eight of the ten living former presidents of the Association made public a letter deploring the "rising crescendo of attacks" on Judge Kaufman over his role in the Rosenberg case. Only Dudley Bonsal, who was a sitting judge, and Herbert Brownell, who had been Attorney General when the final Rosenberg appeals and execution took place, did not sign the letter, essentially recusing themselves. The signatories emphasized that because "[j]udges cannot defend themselves," "it is the duty of the bar to speak up when criticism exceeds bounds of fairness."[53]

Two other Cardozo lectures received wide attention. The Thirty-First Lecture, given by Marvin E. Frankel, then a judge of the Southern District of New York, was entitled "The Search for Truth—An Umpireal View." Frankel's theme was "that our adversary system rates truth too low among the values that institutions of justice are meant to serve." He suggested, "We should begin, as a concerted professional task, to question the premise that adversariness is ultimately and invariably good."[54]

The Thirty-Second Cardozo Lecture, given by Herbert Brownell and entitled "The Forgotten Victims of Crime," was a lecture short on cant and rhetoric, a straightforward talk on how the courts treat the victims of crime as complaining witnesses. Brownell concluded that the criminal justice system is "inadequately prepared to cope with [the victim's] basic physical and psychological needs" and made practical recommendations.[55]

Among others giving important addresses at the Association during this period were Justice William H. Rehnquist, who spoke about the problem of judicial disqualification;[56] Attorney General Edward H. Levi, who spoke on "Confidentiality and Democratic Government";[57] and Milton Handler, who delivered the twenty-fifth and what he announced would be the last of his annual antitrust reviews. Although endowing an annual Milton Handler Lecture on Antitrust at the Association for his successors, he would return again as a speaker.[58]

NOTES

1. Hoffman, *Lions in the Street* (see above, chap. 2, note 4), p. 224; interview with Conrad K. Harper, March 14, 1995.

2. On Schell, see *Women's Wear Daily*, May 21, 1970; *New York Times*, February 6, 1975; *New York Post*, March 22, 1975; interviews with George G. Gallantz (see above, chap. 1, note 3); George Lindsay, March 14, 1995; Robert M. Kaufman (see above, chap. 2, note 56); and Conrad Harper (see above, note 1).

3. See Cyrus R. Vance's "Acceptance of Honorary Membership," in "Presentation of Honorable Membership to the Honorable Cyrus R. Vance," *The Record*, 49 (January/February 1994), 11.

4. See William B. Quandt, *Camp David: Peacemaking and Politics* (Washington, D.C.: Brookings Institution, 1986), pp. 34–35 and passim; Hamilton Jordan, *Crisis: The Last Year of the Carter Presidency* (New York: G. P. Putnam's, 1982), pp. 45–47 and passim.

5. *St. Paul Pioneer Press*, January 14, 1972; *The Record*, 25 (April 1970), 256.

6. The Association's *Scrapbook* for 1970 contains clippings from newspapers located in Asheville, Fresno, Dallas, St. Louis, Bridgeport, Alamogordo, Topeka, Dayton, and Lake Charles, Louisiana, among others.

7. Orville H. Schell, Jr., "Report of the President, 1972–1973," *The Record*, 28 (October 1973), 563, 569–72.

8. *New York Times*, May 3, 1973, reprinted in *The Record*, 28 (June 1973), 402–404.

9. Ibid.

10. *New York Times*, October 25, 1973; *New York Daily News*, October 25, 1973; *New York Post*, October 24, 1973; *New York Times*, October 23, 1973; *National Law Journal*, October 25, 1973.

11. Archibald Cox, "Some Reflections on Possible Abuses of Government Power," *The Record*, 28 (December 1973), 811, 814, 827.

12. *The Record*, 29 (January 1974), 1.

13. See also Committee on Federal Legislation, "The Law of Presidential Impeachment," *The Record*, 29 (February 1974), 154–76, esp. 159.

14. See Association of the Bar of the City of New York, *Scrapbook* for 1974 (available in the library of the Association).

15. *The Record*, 29 (October 1974), 519. The statement was also published in the *New York Law Journal*, September 16, 1974.

16. See, for example, *Washington Star News*, April 18, 1974.

17. Interview with William Hellerstein, vice chair of the Grievance Committee at that time (see above, chap. 2, note 56).

18. *In the Matter of Richard M. Nixon*, 53 A.D.2d 178, 181, 385 N.Y.S. 2d 305, 308 (July 8, 1976).

19. *New York Times*, July 9, 1976.

20. *In the Matter of John Mitchell*, 48 A.D.2d 410 (July 3, 1975).

21. *Harrison* [New York] *Independent*, September 24, 1970; New York *Daily News*, October 16, 1970.

22. *New York Times*, January 26, 1974; February 10, 1974.

23. *Life*, March 12, 1971.

24. *New York Times*, July 3, 1973; Hoffman, *Lions in the Street* (see above, chap. 2, note 4), p. 149; *New York Law Journal*, December 1, 1977.

25. See, for example, Jack B. Weinstein, "The Role of the Chief Judge in a Modern System of Justice," *The Record*, 28 (April 1973), 291.

26. Cynthia Owen Philip, et al., *Where Do Judges Come From?* (New York: Institute of Judicial Administration, 1976), pp. 107ff.

27. See Cyrus R. Vance, "Report of the President, 1975–1976," *The Record*, 31 (October 1976), 415ff.

28. See Committee on State Courts of Superior Jurisdiction, "Legislation Implementing the Court Reform Amendments," *The Record*, 33 (November 1978), 415.

29. Interview with Louis A. Craco (see above, chap 1, note 30).

30. Hoffman, *Lions in the Street* (see above, chap. 2, note 4), pp. 44–45; Cyrus R. Vance, "Report of the President, 1974–75," *The Record*, 30 (October 1975), 471–72; *Torrington* [Connecticut] *Register*, January 23, 1975; *Washington Post*, January 24, 1975; *St. Louis Post-Dispatch*, April 11, 1975.

31. See Vance, "Report of the President, 1975–1976," 439–40 (see above note 27).

32. *New York Times*, April 18, 1975, and February 28, 1978.

33. Richard L. Abel, *American Lawyers* (New York and Oxford: Oxford University Press, 1989), pp. 56, 77, 82.

34. *The Record*, 30 (October 1975), 464–65.

35. Vance, "Report of the President, 1974–75" (see above, note 30), 446–47

36. "Joint Report on the Proposed Rule for Admission to Practice Before the United States District Courts in the Second Circuit," *The Record*, 31 (January/February 1975), 95, 97.

37. *The Record*, 31 (April 1975), 264. On the trial advocacy controversy, see Warren E. Burger, "Some Further Reflections on the Problem of Advocacy of Trial Counsel," *Fordham Law Review*, 49 (1980), 1. See also Marvin E. Frankel, "The Search for Truth—An Umpireal View," *The Record*, 30 (January/February 1975), 14, 28ff.

38. *The Record*, 25 (April 1970), 193–94.

39. Norman Dorsen and Leon Friedman, *Disruption in the Court: Report of the Special Committee on Courtroom Conduct of the Association of the Bar of the City of New York* (New York: Pantheon, 1974). See also *New York Times*, January 13, 1974.

40. *The Record*, 29 (February 1974), 123.

41. *Branzburg v. Hayes*, 408 U.S. 665 (1972).

42. Committee on Federal Legislation, "Journalists' Privilege Legislation," *The Record*, 28 (April 1973), 308.

43. Luther A. Huston, "Conflicting Views Presented at House News Shield Hearings," *Editor and Publisher*, February 17, 1973, p. 9.

44. *The Record*, 29 (January 1974), 87.

45. Committee on Federal Legislation, "On Legislation Enabling Congress to Review and Nullify Executive Impoundment," *The Record*, 28 (June 1973), 508ff.

46. Committee on Federal Legislation, "Gun Control Legislation," *The Record*, 31 (April 1976), 271. See, for example, the use of the committee report by the *Hutchinson* [Kansas] *News*, June 19, 1976.

47. *The Record*, 30 (April 1975), 255; (May/June 1975), 400.

48. Committee on Civil Rights, "The Administration's Proposed Amendment to the Federal Communications Act of 1934, Section 307," *The Record*, 28 (November 1973), 772.

49. Committee on Civil Rights and Committee on International Human Rights, "The Central Intelligence Agency: Oversight and Accountability," *The Record*, 30 (April 1975), 255. See also *New York Law Journal*, April 17, 1975.

50. Committee on Civil Rights, "The Use of Quotas, Goals, and Affirmative Action Programs to Overcome the Effects of Racial Discrimination," *The Record*, 28 (June 1973), 525–26.

51. *The Record*, 29 (February 1974), 128.

52. *The Record*, 34 (March 1979), 157ff.

53. *New York Law Journal*, June 23, 1975.

54. *The Record*, 30 (January/February 1975), 15, 34.

55. The Record, 31 (January 1976), 148.

56. "Sense and Nonsense about Judicial Ethics," *The Record*, 28 (November 1973), 694.

57. *The Record*, 30 (May/June 1975), 175.

58. See *The Record*, 29 (December 1972), 639–41.

4

"Indisputably the Preeminent Center for the Practice of Business and Financial Law in the United States": The Association, Its City, and Its Profession, 1976–80

DURING THE PERIOD BETWEEN May 1976 and May 1980, while the nation dealt with post-Watergate "malaise" and New York City barely survived a financial crisis, the Association, more than during most periods, wrestled with professional matters. During these four years the Association's century-long involvement in lawyer discipline came to an end. Like other bar associations throughout the country, the City Bar was concerned with the problem of lawyer advertising. Perennial problems of judicial administration were also on the Association's platter, as were initiatives in the area of criminal justice. The municipal fiscal crisis was given attention and, during these years, the City Bar also increased its involvement with international human rights. However, in institutional terms, one of the most important things to happen to the Association was the retirement of its Executive Secretary.

INTERNAL DEVELOPMENTS

Paul De Witt retired as Executive Secretary on May 31, 1979. Serving under seventeen presidents, De Witt had been the only Executive Secretary the City Bar had known. His impact had been enormous—over Association policy, style, and product. Adrian De-

Wind, president from 1976 to 1978, elegantly summed up the relationship between De Witt and the City Bar:

> His devotion to and identification with the City Bar were total. He loved the Association; it was his child and his life and no mother hen ever watched more closely over h[er] chick. His sense of the appropriate and his great style were contagious to the officers who came and went over the years. He held sway in his small office off the reception hall and it was a continually convivial spot for so many who dropped in. Paul could be stubborn, cantankerous and demanding. But he also knew how to work with a wide variety of personalities and it was not too often that he did not get his way when he cared.[1]

Though he was deeply involved in every aspect of the Association's work, De Witt's influence was seen in *The Record*, which he edited, in committee appointments, and, most particularly, in the setting of a tone for the Association. Indeed, his involvement in all aspects of the affairs of the Association was so great that even when his health began to fail, his weakening energies still had considerable impact. After he retired as Executive Secretary, De Witt continued to be involved with the Association, taping some seventy cassettes on the history of the organization. He died in 1985.

William Delano was chosen to replace him. Coming from a prominent family, Delano, during the Second World War, had served as a Chinese interpreter in the China–Burma–India theater. After the War, he graduated from Yale College and Law School and served as a civilian volunteer with the American Friends Service Committee. From 1953 to 1961 Delano was an associate of Winthrop Stimson Putnam & Roberts. He then became the first General Counsel of the Peace Corps and, after that, Secretary General of the International Peace Corps. Delano had been active in the Association as a member of the Special Committee to Study Commitment Procedures and the Committee on Sex and Law. He had also been chairman of the Committee on the Bill of Rights and, at the time of his appointment as Executive Secretary, was chair of the Special Committee on the Lawyer's Role in the Search for Peace. Delano had also been very active in civic and philanthropic matters.[2] But his tenure as Executive Secretary would not be long.

The Association continued in these years to grow and to successfully encourage diversity. Membership, which had been 9,294 at the end of Plimpton's first term, was more than 12,000 at the end of Merrell Clark's second term (spring 1980). By 1977 six of the seventeen members of the Executive Committee were either under forty, female, African-American, or some combination thereof.

The financial position of the Association in these years was relatively strained, not only because of the double-digit inflation the country suffered through during these years, but also because of a New York State Court of Appeals decision.

The New York State Constitution provided that "charitable property"—patriotic, literary, medical societies—was not to be taxed. In 1972 the state legislature had passed a law permitting localities to impose real estate taxes on organizations which were not "primarily charitable or educational institutions." New York City then repealed the exemption from property taxes of the House of the Association and that part of the Bar Building used exclusively for Association purposes.[3] In *In the Matter of the Association of the Bar of the City of New York v. Lewisohn* (1974), the Court of Appeals upheld the repeal of the exemption.[4] Counting arrears, the Association owed the City $450,000. Stating that its existence was threatened by the financial crisis, the Association increased dues ten percent and imposed a $75 one-time assessment on all its members.[5] In this way, a difficult situation was eased, but significant improvement in the Association's finances would not occur until the early 1980s when the Bar Building was sold.

One other important internal change took place during this period—the Nominating Committee became independent of the Executive Committee. The Executive Committee had become the Nominating Committee for officers of the Association and members of the Executive Committee in 1972. It did not take long, however, for the Special Committee on the Second Century to recognize that an error had been made—that the mechanism was too ingrown. That committee thought that the "search for well-qualified candidates should be broader in its scope and perhaps more objective in its application." Five of the seats of the new Nominating Committee were to be elected, the one place where competitive elections were built into the process.[6]

A happy ceremonial event was celebrated on March 10, 1980, when the Hughes Room, on the first floor of the House, was dedicated, honoring both Charles Evans Hughes and Charles Evans Hughes, Jr. Chief Justice Warren Burger flew up from Washington for the occasion, and said, in part, of his predecessor as Chief Justice: ". . . he lived his life with grace, poise, integrity, and lived it to the fullest measures. His legacies to our world and to his times were, as we know, rich and many and every American can take pride in that great life."[7]

Finally, the Association cooperated with a sociologist, Michael J. Powell, whose doctoral dissertation and later book would be a sociological analysis of influence in the Association. Powell admitted in the book that he had found the Association's "identity as an upper-class institution much less certain than it had seemed from a distance."[8]

THE PRESIDENTS, 1976–80

From 1976 to 1980, the presidency of the City Bar was held by Adrian W. DeWind and Merrell E. ("Ted") Clark, Jr. Though a well-known tax lawyer with Paul Weiss Rifkind Wharton & Garrison, De-Wind was better known for his involvement with liberal causes. Sixty-two years old when he became president of the Association in 1976, DeWind had been born in Chicago, the son of an engineer. After attending Grinnell College and the Harvard Law School, De-Wind first practiced with the firm of Sage Gray Todd & Sims. He served as Tax Legislative Counsel for the Department of the Treasury (1947–48) before joining Paul Weiss in 1948. Seeing the field of tax law as an intellectual challenge, but also recognizing its "social impact," DeWind began an association with the NAACP Legal Defense and Educational Fund, advising its then director-counsel, Thurgood Marshall, on tax and housing matters. Chief Counsel to the Subcommittee on Administration of the Internal Revenue Laws of the House Ways and Means Committee (1951–52), DeWind has since served on many advisory groups on tax policy—to the President of the United States, the Commissioner of Internal Revenue, and the New York City Council. He has also been active in politics—managing the campaign of Samuel Silverman for Manhattan Surrogate and serving as adviser to Senator Eugene McCarthy in his 1968 run for the Presidency. In his seventies DeWind was still active in liberal causes—as chair of the Natural Resources Defense Council and vice chair of Human Rights Watch and as a director of the Lawyers Alliance for Nuclear Arms Control. DeWind has continued in recent years to be particularly interested in matters of foreign policy and has been a director of the Lawyers' Alliance for World Security. He also serves as a trustee of The New School for Social Research.[9]

Merrell E. ("Ted") Clark, Jr., president of the Association from 1978 to 1980, was born in Brooklyn on April 30, 1922. He attended Yale and Yale Law School where he was an editor of the *Yale Law Journal*. A renowned antitrust litigator with Winthrop Stimson Putnam & Roberts, Clark, unlike DeWind, had been a very active member of the Association before he became president. Clark had been chairman of the Special Committee on the Family Part of the Supreme Court, the Committee on Admissions, the Centennial Committee (1965–70), the Committee on Sex and Law, and the Special Committee on the Second Century. He had also been vice president (1970–73). After his presidency, Clark remained involved with the Association. The most important of his assignments has been as chair of the Committee on Minorities in the Profession. In recent years, he has served as chairman of the Hardship Appeals Panel of the New York City Council, which deals with hardship applications in landmarks preservation matters. He has also chaired the New York City Conflicts of Interest Board and served as Special Master for the National Basketball Association and the Players Union to oversee salary-cap matters. Clark was the fourth member of the Winthrop Stimson firm to head the Association (after Elihu Root, Henry Stimson, and Allen Klots).[10]

THE GRIEVANCE COMMITTEE

The century-old involvement of the Association in lawyer discipline in New York City ended in 1980, the casualty of both national concern over the weak policing of lawyers by lawyers and of more local developments. The Grievance Committee had been one of the glories of the Association. For much of the century, it had been the flagship of lawyer discipline in the United States—praised and respected for professionalism, process, and adequate financing. But by the mid-1970s history had passed it by, and change was inevitable.

The constitution of the Association had given the duty "of the hearing of all complaints against members of this Association" to the Grievance Committee, which was also charged with dealing with all complaints which may be made in "matters affecting the interests of the legal profession and the practice of law and the administration of justice." However, the committee was not active in the very early years of the Association. In 1884 the bylaws were amended to authorize the Association to investigate charges against any member of the bar and, if necessary, to prosecute such an offender. Twelve complaints against lawyers were filed the following year. By 1897 the Association was for the first time providing for a part-time attorney to work with its Grievance Committee. Concurrently, the jurisdiction of the committee was limited to the First Judicial Department—Manhattan and The Bronx. In 1925 a new committee was added, the Committee on Professional Ethics, to address questions about professional conduct directed to it.

In the year immediately preceding Francis Plimpton's first year as president (the year ending April 30, 1968), the Grievance Committee had a staff of six lawyers. At the time, New York City contributed $85,000 of the committee's budget of $200,000. The committee staff had been headed since 1963 by John G. Bonomi—a former assistant district attorney in New York County who had been special counsel to the congressional subcommittee that investigated the links between organized crime and professional boxing—the most highly regarded figure in the nation in the field of attorney discipline. In the year ending April 30, 1968, the Grievance Committee examined 2,483 complaints, taking formal action in 246. During that year, ten lawyers were disbarred by the First Department at the instance of the Grievance Committee; eight suspended; two censured.[11]

For almost a quarter-of-a-century the Association's Grievance Committee was a model for the nation because of its staffing, professionalism, and independence. But allowing a bar association to privately police a public profession went against a national trend. After the Second World War, more and more states had been placing attorney discipline in the hands of independent commissions (often with lay members) directly responsible to state supreme courts. Furthermore, dissatisfaction grew over how few lawyers were actually being punished in New York and the nation. (During the first half of the twentieth century less than one percent of New York City lawyers accused of misconduct received meaningful punishment.[12]) Furthermore, it was the "shyster lawyers," the ambulance chasers, who were punished, never the big corporate types. In 1970 an ABA committee chaired by retired Justice Tom Clark concluded that, in the nation as a whole, there existed "a scandalous situation that require[d] the immediate attention of the profession."[13] Two years later, a committee of the Administrative Board of the New York State Judicial Conference chaired by Marcus G. Christ made a number of recommendations for improvements in the system of attorney discipline in the state (although it did not find "a scandalous situation").

The Special Committee on the Second Century did consider the future of the Grievance Committee in 1974, although its report was relatively superficial. Concerns were expressed about delays, secrecy, and staff turnover, while lay representation on the Grievance Committee and more adequate funding were strongly supported. The Second Century Committee strongly reaffirmed the importance of the work of the committee to the Association: "It is beyond controversy that work in the disciplinary field is among the most important tasks of the Association."[14]

When Cyrus Vance became president of the Association, he appointed an Ad Hoc Committee on Grievance Procedures to review, report on, and make recommendations with respect to, the processing of grievances. The eight-person committee was chaired by Leon Silverman, who had been an Assistant Deputy Attorney General in the Eisenhower Administration. Silverman, then fifty-three years old, was a partner in Fried, Frank, Harris, Shriver & Jacobson and president of The Legal Aid Society. Leslie H. Arps, Eli Whitney Debevoise, George G. Gallantz, and Powell Pierpont were among the other members of the committee. The committee appointed three reporters—Beatrice S. Frank, Alice H. Henkin, and Bruce C. Ratner—who were given authority to read disciplinary files and attend hearings. Their findings would prove important.

The Silverman Committee report was released on February 4, 1976. While the committee reaffirmed the position that the Association should continue to be in the grievance business, it did so with a marked lack of enthusiasm. On the one hand, the Silverman Committee spoke of the Grievance Committee's "reputation for integrity, [its] experience, independence and general competence" and stated that its staff had "maintained a credible grievance system which in the past has been superior to that of other jurisdictions." But the Silverman Committee also found "much that [was] wrong."[15] Delays were serious—averaging two and a half years from the time a complaint was filed until a sanction was imposed by the First Department. The Silverman Committee was critical of the lack of uniform review of staff decisions of the Grievance Committee. In their analysis of particular files, the reporters had pointed to example after example of the dismissal of complaints without investigation because they were "minor fee disputes," although the complaints had alleged far more serious grievances.

The Silverman Committee was disturbed that the Grievance Committee relied so heavily on direct complaints. As a result, serious misconduct of some securities and corporate lawyers was going unpunished. The Silverman Committee worried that there was so much confidentiality that the system was seriously weakened, and was unhappy that there was no public participation in the disciplinary process. The Silverman Committee concluded that "a disciplinary system that moves slowly, and in secret, then ends up publicly disciplining a minuscule percent of those whose conduct is complained about can be neither effective nor credible."[16] Transfer of the disciplinary duties was not recommended, however, because of the "difficulty of finding or quickly creating a new body with the requisite impartiality and integrity."[17]

Every member of the Association received the Silverman Report. There was considerable play in the press. *The Wall Street Journal* of February 4, 1976, exaggerated, but not by much, when it stated that the committee had described the grievance process as slow, superficial, small-minded, and needlessly secret. *The New York Times* made the committee report the subject of a front-page story. A *Times* editorial put a much more generous spin on the report than had *The Wall Street Journal*, stating: "In a remarkably self-critical and constructive report, a prestigious committee of the Association of the Bar of the City of New York calls for tough new ways to censure, discipline or disbar lawyers."[18]

In response to the report, the Association appointed public members to the committee, reorganized the committee and its staff, created new and more flexible disciplinary sanctions, provided more detailed and comprehensive rules of procedure, and added internal review procedures.[19]

The reforms came too late. Not only were national trends against a private association's dominating peer discipline, but there were local factors as well. The image that the Association was unrepresentative of the interests of small practitioners and local lawyers left it vulnerable. A host of scandals involving such major law firms as White & Case, Donovan Leisure and Shea & Gould occurring at the time reinforced the view that it was the transgressions of the "shirt sleeve lawyers" that concerned the Grievance Committee and not those of the "parchment collar lawyers." Among the other elements in the brew was the desire of Francis T. Murphy, who became Presiding Justice of the First Department in the mid-'70s, for more authority over the work of the committee and the fact that an increasing proportion of the costs of the City Bar's participation in the grievance process was publicly funded through contracts between the courts and the Association.

Even so, a 1978 report which was undertaken for the Economic Development Council of New York City, Inc. by a task force headed by Richard F. Coyne saw "significant indications that the Grievance Committee ha[d] 'turned the corner' " with the large number of pending cases, praised the Grievance Committee's "continuing capacity for self-inquiry and attempted self-improvement," and recommended that the Association continue to perform its present functions.[20] But the report could not stop the momentum for divestiture.

The final act took place the following year, when the Appellate

Division asked the Association to transfer the Grievance Committee staff to the state payroll. The First Department believed, not unreasonably, that since the staff was publicly funded, it should be controlled by the appropriate, responsible public agency. The First Department assured the Association that the wishes of the Grievance Committee would be respected as to hiring, firing, promotion, and administration. However, since the appointments to the Grievance Committee itself were being made by the First Department, the Executive Committee saw the result of the proposal as giving the Association only nominal authority. Believing full legal control of the staff essential to continued acceptance of administrative responsibility, the Executive Committee decided to end the long relationship. The announcement was made in March 1980.[21]

THE CHARACTER AND FITNESS PROCESS FOR ADMISSION TO THE NEW YORK BAR

In the mid-1970s, The Association of the Bar of the City of New York and the New York State Bar Association made an unsuccessful attempt to reform the character and fitness process in the state for determining admission to the bar.

That process was the responsibility of each of the four departments of the Appellate Division. In each department, there was a committee of attorneys responsible for determining character and fitness. After passing the bar examination, every applicant for admission in New York State was responsible for filling out an extremely lengthy questionnaire which often intruded on personal privacy. After the questionnaire was filed, each applicant was interviewed by one or more members of the "character committee" of each Department. In 1971 the state's character and fitness mechanisms had barely survived a First Amendment challenge in the U.S. Supreme Court.[22]

A joint committee of the City Bar and the New York State Bar Association undertook a study of the process in New York and issued a scathing report. Perhaps foremost among the objectionable parts of the process, the joint committee pointed out, was that there were no published rules or specific standards. The character committees thus did their work without guidelines as to how prior cases were decided, while applicants were unable to assess what the outcome might be for them.

The eleven-page questionnaire was a monstrosity. It was composed of twenty-eight numbered questions with a myriad of subparts. The applicant was forced to dredge up information on every residence he/she had lived in for more than three months from birth through high school; the names *and relationships* of all persons with whom the applicant was "presently living"; information on schools attended before college; a complete working history from childhood to the present; information on indebtedness of any amount to anyone, on whether the applicant had ever been a *witness* in a judicial proceeding, and whether the applicant had been disciplined by any club, society, or organization. Applicants were also required to file affidavits from past employers as well as affidavits from present members of the New York Bar as to their "good character."

But once the candidate had gathered together all this information, fearful as to what might happen, for example, if he/she were unable to produce the exact address of an apartment he/she had lived in at the age of six, it turned out there was not any way the character committees could check the accuracy of it, because they lacked investigative staff. In point of fact, the information filed was not used by the committees.

The most criticized part of the process was yet to come. That was the personal interview with a member or members of the character committees—committees almost entirely constituted of aged or middle-aged males. No particular expertise was expected of the members appointed to these committees. Of the interviews, the report stated:

> Formal and informal surveys of members of the New York Bar disclose an inexhaustible store of tales as to occurrences during the interview process. Unfortunately, most of the stories do not reflect admirably upon some of the members of the character committees who emerge from these accounts as prejudiced, intrusive, insensitive and frivolous individuals.[23]

For a profession priding itself on its contributions to due process of law, the admission to the bar in New York State was full of irony.

While the number of applicants actually rejected on character grounds was extremely small, the committees dealt with applicants it considered problematic by deferring their decision endlessly, apparently hoping that the applicants would give up. But, even for those whose admission was not delayed, knowledge that such a questionnaire existed chilled word and act from the time of entrance to law school. At least in some cases, the licensing mechanism was being used capriciously to discourage political association or such conduct as men and women living together.

The joint committee recommended limiting the questionnaire to inquiries where answers might lead to disqualification. It cautioned against overly broad inquiries and advocated the elimination of unreasonable intrusions into personal privacy. It urged that requests for documentary back-up be minimized and good moral character affidavits be eliminated. Perhaps most important, on the question of standards, the joint committee thought that:

> Any licensure system with the power of preventing individuals from practicing a chosen livelihood should be governed by relevant standards expressed with clarity. The character investigation system in New York stands in striking contrast to this ideal because of the total absence of state standards for determining when an applicant is unfit to be licensed for the practice of law.[24]

The Appellate Divisions rejected the most sweeping proposals of the committee including those dealing with the interviews and the character affidavits and those proposing drastic reduction in the number of inquiries on the questionnaire. There was progress, however. The questionnaire would be refined and somewhat reduced; procedural rules would be codified and a procedure adopted which permitted a potential applicant to get a preliminary ruling on his/her fitness prior to entering law school.[25]

LAWYER ADVERTISING

In the late 1960s and early 1970s mechanisms long used by the American bar to "protect its turf," which often made it difficult for a consumer to make an informed choice of an attorney, were eroding. By the late 1970s, the most controversial aspect of this problem for bar associations was lawyer advertising. The City Bar took a position that, with only minimal restrictions, supported advertising by lawyers, a position rejected by the New York courts.

Lawyer advertising became a major issue as a result of a series of decisions by the Supreme Court of the United States. The first of these was *Goldfarb v. State Bar*,[26] decided in 1975. The Association prepared an *amicus* brief for *Goldfarb* which argued that uniform fee schedules were a classic example of price-fixing and hence a violation of the antitrust laws. The brief stated that: "Lawyers are not, and should not be, above the law." Ultimately, that is what the Supreme Court held. Commenting on the *Goldfarb* decision, President Vance said, "I think it will further sensitize the bar to its obligation."[27]

Goldfarb was followed by *Bates v. State Bar of Arizona*,[28] in which the Supreme Court invalidated on First Amendment grounds sweeping rules of the State of Arizona against lawyer advertising. Since such sweeping rules existed virtually everywhere, new laws or rules governing advertising by lawyers had to be crafted by legislatures or state supreme courts. In general, those bodies were likely to take the cues of bar associations.

While *Bates* was pending in the Supreme Court, Association committees with jurisdiction over the issue of lawyer advertising were divided. The Committee on Professional Responsibility and the Special Committee on Consumer Affairs filed a joint report favoring very liberal rules, stating that the Association "should support and promote changes in statute, court rule, or bar association code to freely permit truthful and fair advertising by lawyers."[29] But the Committee on Trade Regulation was divided over the issue—half agreed with the joint committee report, half sought a middle ground.[30] President DeWind supported liberalized advertising but, fearful of putting the issue to a referendum of the membership, convinced the Executive Committee to delay action pending the Supreme Court decision in *Bates*.

In the autumn of 1977, the Executive Committee, which included as members Louis Craco, Barry Garfinkel, Conrad Harper, Robert

Kaufman, Leon Silverman, Louis Auchincloss, and Ruth Bader Ginsburg, endorsed an end to all restrictions on advertising except for ads that were "false, fraudulent, misleading or deceptive."[31] That proposal was considered at a special meeting of the Association on February 16, 1978. The meeting must have been lively. Rhoda H. Karpatkin, the chair of the Consumer Affairs Committee, emphasized the consumer stake in lawyer advertising. Sheldon Oliensis, then chair of the Grievance Committee, argued that the Executive Committee proposal presented a straightforward rule that was enforceable. Robert Kasanof, who had dissented within the Executive Committee, expressed doubt that it would be possible to enforce such a broad standard as that proposed by the Executive Committee given the grievance machinery of the time. Philip Anderegg opposed the standard because it was not any higher than general law with respect to fraud and misrepresentation. In contrast, Francis Plimpton stated that he believed that the Executive Committee resolution would allow some lawyers to abuse the opportunity, but he would take a chance on self-restraint by the bar. Judge Aaron Steuer reminded those in attendance that neither alternate proposals nor tabling the Executive Committee proposal for further refinement was practical, because the Appellate Division would act before any new Association standard could be formulated. Finally, the Executive Committee resolution was adopted by a vote of 48 to 18.[32]

In March 1978, the First Department joined the other departments in adopting rules opposed by both the Association and the Department of Justice. The Appellate Division not only prohibited "any public communication containing statements or claims that are false, deceptive, misleading or cast reflection on the legal profession as a whole," but also advertisements containing "puffery, self-laudation, claims regarding the quality of the lawyer's legal service, or claims that cannot be verified."[33]

Nevertheless, developments in the profession came so rapidly that even by January 14, 1979, the debate of just one year before would seem arcane. On that day Jacoby & Myers opened eleven offices in Manhattan, Brooklyn, Queens, and the New York suburbs.

NON-PROFESSIONAL PUBLIC POLICY ISSUES
OF THE LATE SEVENTIES

Judicial Selection, Discipline, and Administration

In the area of judicial administration, the most significant event of the period was the acrimonious debate over the selection of municipal judges, a debate yielding a highly constructive resolution. Both Mayor Robert Wagner (beginning with his last term) and Mayor John Lindsay had agreed to screen all their judicial appointees (to the Criminal and Family Courts) through the Mayor's Committee on the Judiciary and the Association's committees, appointing only those approved by both groups. However, relations between the Association and Abraham Beame, mayor between 1973 and 1977 and much closer to the Democratic organization than his predecessors, were uneasy at best. While Beame was in the midst of an extremely tight race for the Democratic nomination for re-election in 1977, President DeWind joined Robert McKay, then president of The Legal Aid Society, in a statement sharply criticizing the mayor's approach to judicial appointments. "With a few notable exceptions," DeWind and McKay wrote, "the Mayor has not made the best possible appointments but has chosen persons far less able and qualified than he could have chosen and, in some instances, they have been of borderline acceptability." DeWind and McKay pointed out that when a potential Beame appointee was disapproved, the mayor attempted to pressure the Association into approving his choices by refusing to fill the judgeship for years on end. "The Bar Association, it is true, may find the Mayor's choices to be unqualified," De Wind and McKay said. "That is all it can do. It cannot improve on them."[34]

Beame lost the primary and took a measure of revenge. The week after the general election he announced that he would for the remainder of his term fill Criminal and Family Court judgeships without City Bar approval. Just two days before he left office, Beame swore in fifteen "Midnight Judges," a potpourri of relatives of political leaders and ward politicians, six of whom previously had been rejected by the Association and three unscreened. DeWind thundered that the mayor had "succumbed to narrow political considerations in disregard of the tremendous stake the people of New York have in seeing the best possible judges appointed to the courts of the city."[35] Less predictably, the *Philadelphia Inquirer*, the paper of record for a city not unusually distinguished for the quality of its judiciary, headlined its editorial "A N.Y. Judicial Disgrace," calling Beame "arrogant and irresponsible."[36]

There was, however, a happy ending. Mayor-Elect Edward Koch, never shy about making political attacks, called Beame's appointments "an abomination" and promised that he never would appoint a judge found unqualified by the Association *or* the Mayor's Committee—a promise he kept through three terms.[37] Koch still considers his judgeship appointments one of the great accomplishments of his administration—a fair conclusion.

A contretemps between Mayor Koch and the Association did develop, however, precipitated by Bruce Wright. Returned to the Criminal Court in 1978, the irrepressible Wright had celebrated in verse:

> There once was a judge named Wright,
> Whose rulings were quite out of sight;
> No matter how loose
> The conduct of Bruce
> The tabloids were always uptight.
>
> . . . .
> The setting of bail for the poor
> Is like losing the key to the door
> Of Prisons and jails
> For Minority Males
> The addict, the beggar, the whore.[38]

Once again Wright released a defendant accused of a violent crime. Koch sharply criticized Wright. A City Bar committee released a report defending Wright's handling of bail and criticized Koch for his criticism of Wright, although the criticism of Koch was cloaked in praise:

Mayor Koch has consistently made outstanding appointments of the Criminal Court bench. . . . One of the principal dangers of [the appointive system] . . . is the great influence possessed by the appointive power where the judges appointed are subject to reappointment. The Mayor's statement in this case clearly affects the independence of the judiciary.[39]

Koch, of course, disagreed and in the text of a speech prepared for delivery at the Association on November 20, 1979, said he believed it would be "perfectly appropriate on occasions, for me to speak out on specific actions by sitting judges."[40] Wright ran successfully for the Civil Court prior to the expiration of his Criminal Court term.

The equally irrepressible Koch also filed a complaint with the Grievance Committee of the Association during this period against two lawyers who issued a mock subpoena to him for violating the rights of Latinos and blacks.[41]

One of the great successes of the City Bar during the past twenty-five years in the area of state judicial administration was its persuasion of the New York Court of Appeals to permit televised arguments, something that happened with striking rapidity. The idea was James Goodale's, chair of the Special Committee on Communications. On January 25, 1979, the committee unanimously adopted a report recommending that the Court of Appeals permit televising oral argument on an experimental basis. The Association got partial funding from the Ford Foundation and Channel 13, the public television station, to be able to produce and broadcast a full day's argument (eight cases). Goodale, his friend Fred Friendly, and Merrell Clark personally appeared before the judges on June 22, 1979, and "made their pitch," which turned out to be an easy sell. The taping occurred on October 16, 1979. The finished tape was given a special preview at the Association on January 23, 1980. Chief Judge Lawrence H. Cooke spoke at that session, and counsel in some of the televised cases commented.[42]

Criminal Justice

Association interest in matters of criminal justice was reinvigorated during the 1970s. Perhaps the most important efforts had to do with proposals for draconian anti-drug legislation. The Committee on Criminal Courts, Law and Procedure strongly opposed the tough anti-drug legislation pushed by Governor Nelson Rockefeller, the original draft of which prohibited plea bargaining and provided for mandatory life sentences for adult drug pushers and addicts who committed crimes. The committee described the proposal as "conceptually barbaric, incompatible with the entire structure and approach of New York's modern penal law and in some respects preposterous to the point of unconstitutionality."[43] The law that eventually was adopted, which displeased the committee only a little less, provided for mandatory life sentences for drug pushers with eligibility for parole only after a minimum prison term and even then only with lifelong parole supervision.

At least one of the reasons the Association opposed the Rockefeller legislation was the judgment that it would not work. Several years after the laws went into effect, the Association, in conjunction with the Drug Abuse Council, undertook an evaluation of the experience with the laws, an evaluation published as a book.[44] The study, reported nationwide in the press, found that the tough law seemed not to have had the intended deterrent effect. The use and availability of drugs in New York State had not been reduced. Not only were the courts more overloaded, because those charged with offenses had no incentive to plea bargain, but there had in fact been fewer dispositions, convictions, and prison sentences under the new law. Shortly thereafter, the New York State Legislature rewrote the state drug law reducing considerably the mandatory penalties. The City Bar study provided the legislature with the data it needed to justify revision of the law.[45]

THE ASSOCIATION AND THE NEW YORK CITY FISCAL CRISIS OF THE 1970S

What may have been the gravest crisis to confront the City of New York during the twentieth century began in February 1974 when the State Urban Development Commission defaulted on an issue of notes after its underwriters were unwilling to roll them over. Concerned about the viability of other New York governmental entities, the financial community refused to roll over New York City's municipal debt in a new loan. As a result, New York City and the New York City Housing Authority lost access to the bond markets. During the next five years, as the City sought first to avoid bankruptcy and then to reclaim its financial autonomy, the Association was supportive of the city, while strongly recommending reform of local financial practices. Many of the proposals put forward by the City Bar's Committee on Municipal Affairs during this period ultimately were adopted.[46]

The seeds of New York City's fiscal crisis were sown in the early 1960s, when the City began to finance its annual budget deficits by borrowing. The City depleted its reserve funds and issued short-term notes to balance its budget, borrowing in anticipation of revenues from the following year. It was but a short step to borrowing on the basis of over-optimistic revenue projections. When the anticipated revenues did not come in, notes were rolled over. Then, in the early 1970s the Local Finance Law of New York State was amended to permit various kinds of borrowing for current expenses. The result of all this was a huge cumulative deficit. By 1975, the total City debt was $11 billion ($6.8 billion long-term). The City had long-term financing needs of $500 million quarterly for capital and operating expenses and short-term financial needs of $750 million monthly. Not only was the investing public's ability to evaluate the City's finances distorted by these years of financial mismanagement, with their dubious accounting practices, poor internal controls, and lack of disclosure, but the public officials themselves also were taken in by what they had unleashed or permitted to happen.

As the crisis worsened in late 1975 and the Ford Administration showed little disposition to help, Cyrus Vance and Robert McKay (then chair of the Executive Committee) urged in forceful language that the federal government take all necessary steps to prevent municipal bankruptcy. The two men wrote:

> As lawyers we are familiar with the complexities of large commercial bankruptcies. The complexity and magnitude of a municipal bankruptcy proceeding involving the City of New York, however, staggers the imagination. At the very minimum resolution of all the contested

issues would produce thousands of costly lawsuits, clogged courts and interminable delays.

No one but the army of lawyers who would be employed to grapple with these problems would have anything to gain. Lawyers don't need this. Neither does the city, which is making a strenuous effort to put its house in order.

The bankruptcy of New York City should be avoided if humanly possible. Federal policy should be designed to help New York restore its credit, not to allow bankruptcy to harm its credit. We believe that the better, the less costly, indeed the humane solution, is a federal guarantee coupled with appropriate conditions and controls.[47]

The city survived the crisis with a moratorium on debt repayment (later declared unconstitutional), by creation of the Municipal Assistance Corporation, which could pledge sales tax revenue to secure bonds, and creation of Emergency Financial Control Boards, which took over financial affairs for the city government, mandated budgetary cuts, and imposed other restraints.

During the parlous times which followed, Adrian DeWind, president as of 1976, performed two important services. First, he chaired a Special Task Force on taxation for the Municipal Assistance Corporation which recommended controversial revisions in state and local taxes to stem the exodus of business and jobs from the city.[48] Then, at a time when municipal morale was at a very low ebb and the city in disrepute throughout the country, DeWind, representing at that moment the establishment bar, spoke out loudly about the significance of New York City to lawyers (and, indeed, to all Americans). This is part of what he said:

New York City is indisputably the preeminent center for the practice of business and financial law in the United States. . . . There are more lawyers with greater depth in ability, experience and sophistication practicing business and financial law in the City of New York than anywhere else in the country.

As a great port city and commercial, cultural, scientific and educational center, New York should surely have a strong legal community. However, the basic reason for New York's preeminence is a simple one. The City is the national and international banking and financial center for the country. As such it has attracted to itself and its environs an unparalleled concentration of major corporate headquarters.

But New York's banks, investment houses, stock and commodity exchanges, brokerage firms, insurance companies and other capital institutions bring not only the corporate headquarters. They are also the key to thousands and thousands of important transactions each year that require extensive and expert legal service.[49]

During this period the City Bar was a constructive voice for reform of the financial practices of the city government. The Committee on Municipal Affairs, first chaired by George H. P. Dwight, and its Subcommittee on Local Finances (whose members included Paul Crotty, Milton Mollen, Edward Costikyan, and Edith Spivack and whose chairman was Evan Davis) studied the debt, budget, and disclosure practices of the city. The committee recommended basic revisions to the Local Finance Article of the state constitution, a law to make full disclosure the policy of the state and a new mechanism for state oversight and enforcement of balanced budget requirements. Many of the proposals were eventually adopted.[50]

In addition, the Committee on Labor and Social Security Legislation made a series of reports on the impact of the fiscal crisis on collective bargaining. It analyzed the roles of the Emergency Financial Control Board, the mayor, and the state legislature in determining the wages, hours, and working conditions of New York City employees and considered the effects of litigation and federal intervention. The implications for the Board of Education, the Board of Higher Education, and the Health and Hospitals Corporation were also assessed.[51]

INTERNATIONAL HUMAN RIGHTS: THE MISSION TO ARGENTINA

One of the most notable activities of the Association during its fifth quarter-of-a-century has been the missions to foreign countries to investigate and report on allegations of gross abuses of human rights, particularly as they relate to the system of justice and the rule of law. Three to five lawyers usually spend from four to ten days in the country being investigated, meeting with members of the local bar and judiciary, visiting prisoners detained for political offenses and, when possible, seeing high officials of the host government and U.S. diplomatic officials. Following the visit, a report is prepared, which often has been published in *The Record* and distributed to members of Congress, the press, and the public. Over the past twenty-five years, missions have gone to such countries as South Korea, the Philippines, Malaysia, and Singapore; Kenya and Uganda; Turkey and Yugoslavia; Northern Ireland; El Salvador and Guatemala; Chile and Argentina. Orville Schell, Adrian DeWind, Robert McKay, Sheldon Oliensis, Beatrice Frank, Marvin Frankel, and William Hellerstein are among those who have undertaken these missions. While it is impossible to accurately assess the value of these missions (which have been funded by grants), they often have provoked great debate within the host country, have given hope and comfort to leading dissidents, may have offered some asssurance of physical safety, and sometimes have led to the release of prisoners. In one case, Malaysia, the concerns expressed by the Association and the bars of other countries may well have prevented the destruction of the independence of the national bar.[52]

Each one of the reports from these missions bears reading, but one of the most compelling is that of the 1979 mission to Argentina that was headed by Orville Schell, a report which evokes that nightmarish atmosphere of Latin American authoritarianism described so vividly in the works of novelists such as Donoso and Dorfman of Chile, Martinez Moreno of Uruguay, and Sabato and Costantini of Argentina.[53]

The Argentine mission was undertaken three years after a military junta had assumed control of the government. That coup had occurred in the wake of strident political demonstrations and terrorist attacks from left and right—the latter operating with at least tacit government consent. Once the new junta assumed power, it commenced a "dirty war" against all types of "subversion." Thousands of citizens were arrested. Many thousands of others disappeared, never to return. This is how it was described in the mission's report:

> There is no question that since March 24, 1976, groups of armed people serving in military, police or other state security forces have ab-

PRESIDENTS OF THE ASSOCIATION,
1968 to Present

Francis T. P. Plimpton, 1968–1970

Bernard Botein, 1970–1972

Orville H. Schell, Jr., 1972–1974
(*painting by Daniel E. Greene*)

Cyrus R. Vance, 1974–1976

Adrian W. DeWind, 1976–1978

Merrell E. Clark, Jr.,
1978–1980 (*painting by
Everett Raymond Kinstler*)

Oscar M. Ruebhausen, 1980–1982

Louis A. Craco, 1982–1984
(*painting by Everett Raymond Kinstler*)

Robert B. McKay, 1984–1986
(*painting by Everett
Raymond Kinstler*)

Robert M. Kaufman, 1986–1988
(*photo by Bachrach*)

Sheldon Oliensis, 1988–1990

Conrad K. Harper, 1990–1992
(*photo copyright Brooks/Glogan
Photographers*)

John D. Feerick, 1992–1994 (*photo by Ken Levinson*)

Barbara Paul Robinson, 1994–1996 (*photo by Bachrach*)

Michael A. Cardozo, 1996–
(*photo by David Lubarsky*)

ducted thousands of people, subjecting most of the victims to torture, killing many, holding others in concentration camps or other secret places, and withholding from their families and all the world word either of their whereabouts or whether they remain alive. . . .

The grim and familiar pattern of these disappearances, with variations in detail, was recounted to us by relatives of the *desaparecidos* (the disappeared), as well as by some who disappeared and were lucky enough later to "reappear". A group of armed people in civilian clothes arrives in unmarked automobiles at the home or office of the person or persons to be abducted. Others may be taken from the streets or from other public places. The armed assailants often identify themselves as security officers. No uniformed police or military personnel makes any pretense of interfering with the abductions.[54]

The mission met with the Argentine Minister of Justice, the president of the Supreme Court of Argentina, the commander-in-chief of the army (a member of the Junta) and legal advisers to the president. They were not able to meet with the Minister of Interior, visit any prisoners, or confer with Jacobo Timerman, the former editor of *La Opinion*, to whose ultimate freedom the mission contributed.[55]

The report concluded: "[I]f degradations of this kind are utterable, the cases of the 'disappeared' persons constitute the most starkly brutal human rights violations in Argentina or, indeed, almost anywhere in the world that seeks to be civilized."[56] Appended to the report were lists of detained lawyers and "Disappeared Lawyers"—ninety-two in the latter category from Raoul Hugo Alais to José Alfredo Zelayarnass.

Finding some lawyers too cowed to speak up and the "Establishment Bar Association" not dissatisfied with developments, the members of the mission (who also included Marvin Frankel; Harold H. Healy, former Secretary of the Association; Stephen Kass, chair of the Committee on Inter-American Affairs; and R. Scott Greathead, a member of the Committee on International Human Rights) wrote:

When governments brutalize their citizens, depriving them of life, liberty and even the pretext of due process of law, lawyers must stand with those deprived of their rights regardless of our agreement or disagreement with their political or social views. Where the bar most directly involved is itself too threatened to act, lawyers elsewhere must speak for their colleagues and remind those responsible that humanity is extinguished, not advanced, by murder, torture and imprisonment without trial. If, in a different time and place, our circumstances were reversed with those of our Argentine colleagues, we would expect no less of them.[57]

When the mission returned, it briefed delegates of the Organization of American States who were intending to visit Argentina. Schell and Frankel testified at congressional hearings. Members of the mission met with Deputy Secretary of State Warren Christopher a year later to express their concern over reports that the United States was easing its stand on human rights in Argentina. They seem to have been satisfied by what they heard.[58]

THE WORK OF THE COMMITTEE ON FEDERAL LEGISLATION

Between 1976 and 1980, the Committee on Federal Legislation, chaired first by John Feerick and then by Steven Rosenfeld, was involved with a great many important subjects. The committee recommended against a national direct primary, but supported congressional regulation of the timing of presidential primaries in the states that choose to hold them, without taking a stand as to the desirability of regional primaries or just limiting the number of days on which elections would be held. The committee supported ending the electoral college and having direct election of the President.[59]

The committee disagreed with Chief Justice Burger and many others when it opposed an end to federal diversity jurisdiction.[60] The committee took an expansive approach to citizen standing, recommending a law which in essence declares that every citizen who seeks to challenge illegal or unconstitutional government conduct be granted standing to sue to the fullest extent permitted by Article III of the Constitution.[61]

The Committee on Federal Legislation also favored restrictions on law enforcement and intelligence agencies. In a forty-five–page report entitled "Legislative Control of the FBI," the Committee concluded that the FBI's domestic intelligence activities ought to be restricted to the investigation of violations of federal law and that it should be prohibited from monitoring the political activities of individuals and groups; that a judicial warrant based upon a showing of "probable cause" should be required for electronic surveillance, mail covers and openings, and the new targeting of informers.[62]

The Committee was sharply critical of proposals for a constitutional amendment requiring a balanced budget, stating:

> We take no position on the economic issue of whether the federal budget should be balanced or federal spending limited. We do, however, strongly believe, assuming a balanced budget is desirable, a constitutional amendment requiring that result is not. To elevate such a policy to permanent constitutional status is unwise and historically unsound and would fundamentally alter the principle of majority rule and the existing allocation of powers among the three branches of government. In our judgment, the economic policy issues raised in the current debate are best left to the political process where they can be resolved over time, unhampered by fixed or arbitrary constitutional structures.[63]

NOTES

1. Adrian W. DeWind, "[Remarks on] Paul Burton De Witt, 1910–1985," *The Record*, 41 (January/February 1986), 50, 64.
2. *The Record*, 34 (May/June 1979) 326–27.
3. Botein, "Report of the President, 1970–71" (see above, chap. 2, note 5), 507.
4. *New York Times*, May 9, 1974.
5. Ibid., October 9, 1974.
6. Special Committee on the Second Century, "The Selection of the Nominating Committee," *The Record*, 29 (December 1974), 707.
7. "Dedication of the Hughes Room by the Honorable Warren E. Burger, March 10, 1980," *The Record*, 35 (March 1980), 95.
8. Powell, *From Patrician to Professional Elite* (see above, chap. 1, note 2), p. xvii.
9. Biographical information on DeWind came from interviews with DeWind himself (see above, chap. 1, note 31), George G. Gallantz (see above, chap. 1, note 3), George Lindsay (see above, chap. 3, note 2), and Conrad Harper (see above, chap. 3, note 1). In addition, see Hoffman, *Lions in the Street* (see above, chap. 2, note 4), pp. 116–18, and the *New York Post*, May 28, 1976.
10. *New York Times*, April 25, 1978.
11. Martin, *Causes and Conflicts* (see above, chap. 1, note 22), pp. 353, 378.

12. Abel, *American Lawyers* (see above, chap. 3, note 33), p. 145.

13. A.B.A. Special Committee on Evaluation of Disciplinary Enforcement, Problems and Recommendations in Disciplinary Enforcement (June 1970), p. 1.

14. Special Committee on the Second Century, "The Committee on Grievances" (see above, chap. 1, note 35).

15. Association of the Bar of the City of New York, Report of the Ad Hoc Committee on Grievance Procedures (1976), p. 4.

16. Ibid., p. 16. See also pp. 3; 4; 11, note 25; 28–32; 39.

17. Ibid., p. 3.

18. The news story was in the *New York Times*, February 4, 1976. The editorial was in the issue of February 6, 1976.

19. Letter to the *New York Times* of Merrell E. Clark, Jr., and Lola S. Lea, published March 2, 1979.

20. Economic Development Council of New York City, Inc. Task Force, "Analysis of the Grievance System of The Association of the Bar of the City of New York," *The Record*, 34 (November 1979), 561, 565.

21. Powell, *From Patrician to Professional Elite* (see above, chap. 1, note 2), p. 148.

22. *Law Students Civil Rights Research, Inc. v. Wadmond*, 410 U.S. 154 (1971).

23. Special Committee on Professional Education and Admissions of The Association of the Bar of the City of New York and Committee on Legal Education and Admissions to the Bar of the New York State Bar Association, "The Character and Fitness Committees in New York State," *The Record*, 33 (January/February 1978), 20. See also 26, 29, 35, 37. Marvin E. Frankel chaired the Association committee; Thomas M. Hampson, the state bar committee.

24. Ibid., 37.

25. Powell, *From Patrician to Professional Elite* (see above, chap. 1, note 2), pp. 150–55.

26. 421 U.S. 773 (1975).

27. Vance, "Report of the President, 1975–1976" (see above, chap. 3, note 27), 447–48; *New York Times*, February 24, 1975. The High Court rejected the City Bar's attempt to file the brief.

28. 433 U.S. 350 (1977).

29. "Advertising by Lawyers," *The Record*, 32 (March 1977), 114.

30. Committee on Trade Regulation, "Lawyer Advertising and the Antitrust Laws—A Search for a New Solution," *The Record*, 32 (April 1977), 190.

31. *New York Law Journal*, October 17, 1977.

32. Minutes of a Special Meeting of the Association, Thursday, February 16, 1978, *The Record*, 33 (March 1978), 100; New York *Daily News*, February 17, 1978.

33. *New York Law Journal*, February 23, 1978, and March 15, 1978.

34. *New York Law Journal*, August 23, 1977; *New York Times*, August 23, 1977; *Troy Times Record*, August 23, 1977.

35. *New York Law Journal*, December 29, 1977.

36. *Philadelphia Inquirer*, December 31, 1977.

37. *Syracuse Herald Journal*, December 30, 1977; *New York Post*, December 29, 1977; *New York Times*, December 30, 1977.

38. *New York Post*, March 1, 1978.

39. *New York Law Journal*, July 19, 1979.

40. *New York Law Journal*, November 21, 1979. On the Wright–Koch episode, see *New York Times*, February 28, 1978; *New York Daily World*, July 20, 1979.

41. *New York Times*, September 5, 1979.

42. Interview with Merrell E. Clark, Jr. (see above, chap. 1, note 8); *The Record*, 34 (November 1979), 537; Lawrence H. Cooke, "Television Experiment of the New York Court of Appeals," *The Record*, 35 (January/February 1980), 5.

43. *New York Times*, March 1, 1973.

44. Joint Committee on New York Drug Law Evaluation, *The Nation's Toughest Drug Law: Evaluating the New York Experience* (New York: Association of the Bar of the City of New York, 1977).

45. Powell, *From Patrician to Professional Elite* (see above, chap. 1, note 2), pp. 243, 244, 248. See also *Honolulu Advertiser*, September 6, 1976; *New York Times*, July 18, 1978; *New York Times*, September 5, 1976.

46. Interview with Evan Davis (see above, chap. 1, note 31).

47. *The Record*, 20 (December 1975), 616–18. See also *New York Law Journal*, November 10, 1975.

48. *New York Times*, May 26, 1976.

49. Adrian DeWind, "For Legal Profession, New York Is Preeminent as Center of Activity," *New York Law Journal*, June 27, 1977.

50. Committee on Municipal Affairs, "Proposals to Strengthen the Local Finance Laws in New York State," *The Record*, 34 (January/February 1979), 58ff.

51. The first report was "Impact of the Fiscal Crisis and the State Emergency Act on the Structure and Scope of Collective Bargaining," *The Record*, 31 (May/June 1976), 386ff.

52. Interview with John D. Feerick (see above, chap. 1, note 2); Sidney S. Rosdeitcher, "The Bar Association as a Model Non-Governmental Organization: The Rule of the Bar Association in Maintaining an Effective Independent Bar," p. 14 (unpublished manuscript on file in the library of the Association); Marvin L. Frankel, remarks at Stated Meeting of November 18, 1980, Minutes, pp. 62–63.

53. "Report of the Mission of Lawyers to Argentina, April 1–7, 1979," *The Record*, 34 (October 1979), 473.

54. Ibid., 483.

55. *White Plains Reporter-Dispatch*, April 8, 1979; *Washington Post*, April 8, 1979.

56. "Report of the Mission of Lawyers to Argentina" (see above, note 53) 483.

57. Ibid., 491.

58. *The Record*, 35 (October 1980), 366–67.

59. Committee on Federal Legislation, "The Revision of the Presidential Primary System," *The Record*, 33 (May/June 1978), 306; Committee on Federal Legislation, "Proposed Constitutional Amendment Providing for Direct Election of President and Vice President," *The Record*, 33 (May/June 1978), 335.

60. Committee on Federal Legislation, "Federal Diversity Jurisdiction," *The Record*, 33 (November 1978), 493.

61. Committee on Federal Legislation and Committee on the Federal Courts, "Citizens' Standing to Sue in Federal Courts," *The Record*, 34 (November 1979), 585, 601.

62. *The Record*, 32 (May/June 1977), 264.

63. Committee on Federal Legislation, "Budget-Balancing by Constitutional Amendment," *The Record*, 34 (May/June 1977), 428.

5

"In the Real Estate and Construction Business for a While": The Association in the Early 1980s

THE EARLY 1980s were a period of important change in the life of the Association. During this period the *pro bono* mission of the Association deepened, and the Association reached out, not only to women and minorities, but to the local and specialty bars as well. There were also important internal developments. The House was renovated; the Bar Building sold, and the Association placed on a much stronger financial footing. During this period Fern Schair began her tenure as Executive Secretary. For many, it was during these years that the Association became a much less formidable place.

THE PRESIDENTS

Oscar Ruebhausen and Louis Craco served as presidents between 1980 and 1984. Ruebhausen, a partner in Debevoise & Plimpton, may have been the most able manager of internal Association matters of any president during the Association's fifth quarter-of-a-century. Ruebhausen graduated from Dartmouth College and Yale Law School, where he was notes editor of the law review. Immediately after law school he became an associate with Debevoise & Plimpton (then known as Debevoise Stevenson Plimpton & Page). In 1942 he went to Washington, as an attorney with the Lend-Lease Administration. From 1944 to 1946 he served as General Counsel for the Office of Scientific Research and Development. In 1946 he returned to

Debevoise & Plimpton as a partner where he remained until his retirement from law practice in 1987. In 1950–51 he briefly re-entered government service as counsel to the International Development Advisory Board, created to implement a program of assistance to what was then described as the underdeveloped world. President Truman named Nelson Rockefeller as chairman of this Board, and that association with the future governor began for Ruebhausen a close professional and personal relationship of nearly thirty years. While Rockefeller was governor, Ruebhausen served him in many ways, including as chairman of a Task Force on Protection from Radioactive Fallout, as Special Advisor on Atomic Energy, and as chairman of a special panel on Insurance Holding Companies. During this period he also served as chairman of the Board of Bennington College for eleven years and, later, as chairman of the Board for the Russell Sage Foundation for nearly fifteen years. At the Association, Ruebhausen was a member of its Admissions Committee in the late '40s and, for an unusually long period of time, was chair of influential Association committees concerned with the interaction of law and science. He was chair of the Special Committee on Atomic Energy from 1949 to 1959 and of the Committee on Science and Law from 1959 to 1967. As president of the Association, Ruebhausen set the wheels rolling for the rehabilitation of the House, a rehabilitation he would oversee during Louis Craco's presidency. He also upgraded the administrative staff, moving the Association "forward to a much more effective organization than it had been before."[1] Deciding that the chair of the Executive Committee and the president should work closely together, Ruebhausen leaned very heavily on Robert Kaufman during his first term and was supported strongly by Archibald Murray during his second. He also enlarged the traditional role of Association vice presidents and brought his own vice presidents, Judah Gribetz and Harold Tyler, actively into the work of the president's office. After completing his term as president, Ruebhausen served as chairman of the Commission on College Retirement, a commission created by four major foundations, under the leadership of the Carnegie Corporation, to study and report on retirement and pension policies for college and university personnel.[2]

The youngest person ever to head the Association (and the first

Italian Catholic), Louis Craco was born in New York City on October 18, 1933. He attended Holy Cross College and New York University Law School. A partner at Wilkie Farr & Gallagher, Craco was chair of the Association's Committee on Civil Rights (1965–69), secretary of the Association (1969–71), member of the Committee on the Judiciary and then of the Executive Committee. He was chairman of the Executive Committee during the first year Merrell Clark was president and, later, chairman of the Council on Criminal Justice. An articulate and dynamic man, Craco was chair, from 1965 to 1968, of the Mayor's Task Force on Reorganization of New York City Government. Craco's great achievement as president would be to greatly increase the amount of *pro bono* work of the private bar through the creation of VOLS, the Volunteers of Legal Service.

INTERNAL DEVELOPMENTS DURING THE
RUEBHAUSEN–CRACO PERIOD

Fern Schair

William Delano's tenure as Executive Secretary was short. There were staff problems, complaints from the committee chairs, long delays in publication of *The Record* and the *Yearbook*. Delano did not work well with Ruebhausen, a first-rate administrator who was deeply involved in managing the internal affairs of the Association. A request from Delano for a steep salary increase provoked a review of his performance by a committee appointed by the chairman of the Executive Committee, Robert Kaufman. The committee was chaired by Judah Gribitz and included Archibald Murray, Judith Kaye, George Ashley, and Philip Potter. Delano resigned by Labor Day, 1981.

Everyone now claims credit for the selection of Fern Schair as the Association's third Executive Secretary. In fact, the selection committee which chose Schair comprised Ruebhausen (chair), Robert Kaufman, Cyrus Vance, and Archibald Murray. In advertising for the position, the Association had said that it was: ". . . looking for a lawyer who is interested in issues of legal policy, enjoys working with people, has an aptitude for writing and skill in supervising the work of others."[3] Many applied and a number were interviewed, but, according to Murray, when they interviewed Schair "they looked at each other and realized that this was it, precisely the right person with the right mix of experience and people skills."[4]

Schair is a native of Queens and a graduate of St. John's University School of Law. She practiced with The Legal Aid Society of Westchester and for six years was director of the Fund and Committee for Modern Courts, where she wrote extensively on issues of court reform. (Robert MacCrate claims credit for hiring her for the Fund.[5]) As a member of the Association, Schair had served as member of the Civil Court Committee and chair of its subcommittee on pre-recorded video-taped trials. At the time of her appointment as Executive Secretary, Schair was on the board of the Citizens Union and the Fortune Society, and a member of the Statewide Task Force on Courthouse Facilities and of the Westchester Task Force on Jail Overcrowding.[6]

When Schair took over on June 18, 1982, the Association had 13,000 members and 97 committees. Schair has had an enormous amount to do with the growth and vitality of the Association since then and with the deepening of its missions. The Executive Secretary has responsibilities for the substantive programs of the Association, the work of the committees, the Association's relations with its members, and its presence in the community.[7] Virtually everyone who has worked with Schair lauds her enthusiasm, vitality, and people skills. Some examples: The first president to serve a full term with Schair, Louis Craco, speaks of her sense of humor, her ability as quick study, and her ability to manage her many different roles.[8] Cyrus Vance has spoken of his "joy" to have worked with her, "without whose wisdom and matchless skills this Association could not have reached and maintained its remarkable level of achievement and service to the legal community and beyond."[9] Robert Kaufman refers to her "great talent, wisdom, judgment, perception and tact;"[10] Conrad Harper, to her "quick and infectious sense of humor, her remarkable powers of analysis," and "her perspicuity wrapped in humor."[11] Still another president said, "Fern is the organization."[12]

Besides Schair, there was other recasting of the administrative staff of the Association during the Ruebhausen presidency. Prior to Schair's appointment, the position of Executive Administrator had been created to deal with internal business and administrative affairs (physical facilities, purchasing, budgetary services). Grady E. Jensen, who had had extensive experience in administrative management and been mayor of Scarsdale, was named to that position in March 1981. When Gerald T. MacDonough retired in September 1983 after thirty years' service as Administrative Manager (housekeeping, catering, mailings, personnel, security, office equipment), he was succeeded on October 1, 1983, by Gene F. Waters, who had been with the Association since 1964, and there was a recasting of the functions of that office. The new position of Personnel Manager was created at that time. At the end of the Ruebhausen presidency, Otto G. Gara was named the first Associate Librarian, and the position of Counsel in the office of the Executive Secretary was also created.

The second Counsel (later General Counsel—the title was changed in 1994), Alan Rothstein, appointed in the fall of 1985, would become an important force in the life of the Association. Rothstein, a graduate of City College, Brown University (where he earned a Masters Degree in economics), and New York University Law School, had worked as an economist in the public and the private sector, practiced law with Weil Gotshal & Manges, and served as an Associate Director and Counsel to Citizens Union.

More personnel changes—through retirements and the creation of new positions—would occur during Craco's presidency and early in Robert McKay's. Fred Baum would become Director of Library Services; Linda Largi, Director of Membership Services; Susan Narod, Director of Public Information; Scott W. Steffey, Legislative Coordinator; Allan Charne, Executive Director of the Legal Referral Service. By 1985, the only key members of the staff whose tenure in office pre-dated Ruebhausen's presidency were Anthony P. Grech, Librarian and Curator, and Ann M. Cafferty, Controller.[13]

Among the other changes of the Ruebhausen presidency were the computerization of membership records; the printing of *The Record* on a computerized letterpress (beginning with the May 1981 issue), and the updating and modernizing of the bylaws, which included making them gender-neutral.[14]

THE SALE OF THE BAR BUILDING AND THE
RENOVATION OF THE HOUSE

In a report on "The Financial Affairs of the Association" published
in 1974, the Special Committee on the Second Century had reported:

> Recent Presidents of the Association explored imaginative programs
> involving the utilization of parcels adjoining the House of the Associa-
> tion or the Bar Building and the erection of a new large structure . . .
> which would furnish the Association with needed new space and an
> important revenue base. None of these projects could be brought to
> fruition. . . .[15]

Among the projects referred to was the consideration given during
Russell Niles's presidency to buying the hotel adjoining the House
and the discussions during the DeWind presidency relating to the
possible move of the U.S. Court of Appeals for the Second Circuit to
the Bar Building.

The Association had owned the fourteen-story Bar Building at 36
West 44th Street next door to the House since it had built it in the
1920s, when it had consolidated the land from a number of smaller
buildings. The Bar Building permitted the Association to have direct
access to additional space on contiguous floors, but hopes that it
would also become a substantial revenue producer were never borne
out.

The House on 44th Street, built in 1896, was the Association's
third home. The first building at 20 West 27th Street, purchased in
May 1870, had a basement and four floors. The second house was
created in 1882 from the buildings at 3, 5, and 7 West 29th Street.
The 44th Street House, designed by Cyrus L. W. Eidlitz, cost
$640,000—for land, building, and furnishings.[16] After the Second
World War, two large-scale renovations took place—one under Harrison Tweed (begun in 1946) and one for the library in the late 1950s.
The House was also refurbished during the centennial, but some
planned rehabilitation was not done as unexpected expenses were
incurred to protect the meeting hall from an accumulation of mois-
ture. The House had been designed in 1896 for a membership of

1,500. In 1981, the membership was 13,000, and the Association was using 40,000 square feet of the 140,000 in the Bar Building for office space and library book-storage.

There was renewed consideration of what to do with the House and Bar Building early in the Ruebhausen presidency. Ravitch and Rose, real estate consultants, were hired in December 1980. In 1981, the Association acquired a ninety-nine-year lease on land to the east of the Bar Building on 43rd Street. The plan that evolved had as its centerpiece the sale of the Bar Building, with the proceeds to be used both for renovation of the House and for endowment.

In March 1982 the Association contracted to sell the Bar Building and its interest in the lease on the improved land on 43rd Street. The contract was negotiated under the supervision of the Ad Hoc Committee on the Association's Development Program chaired by Ruebhausen. The financing was creative. The aggregate purchase price of the Bar Building was $14.2 million. The Bar Building was leased briefly prior to sale at a rent of $350,000 per year, while the Association retained rent-free the space it had been occupying in the building. At the time the sale was consummated $4.2 million was paid in cash, and the Association was given a $10 million first mortgage, with a net return on the mortgage increasing from ten percent to twelve percent after three years. Thus, after sale, the annual net cash yield from the Bar Building was several times greater than the rents would have been on the building had the Association retained it. The Association also retained a right of refusal on up to 20,000 feet of additional space in the building.

With the deal made, the Association in the spring of 1982 launched a multimillion-dollar renovation of the House. James Stewart Polshek and Partners, who were renovating Carnegie Hall at the time, were hired to prepare a master plan for the restoration of the House to its original appearance and distinction, while providing additional usable space. The firm then carried out the restoration.

The renovation increased the usable square footage of the House and reduced from 40,000 to 10,000 square feet the space used in the Bar Building, most of which was in the basement where it was leased perpetually without charge and used for stacks. The restoration provided for the closed book stacks, which had been scattered in eleven different nooks and crannies, to be consolidated in the basement of the House and the Bar Building. More reading room and stack space was provided within the library, and the vaulted library clerestory windows were restored. Two new meeting rooms were added to the first floor and the other rooms restored and refurbished. On the first floor, the reception area was also improved. The Great Hall was redecorated and provided with new light and sound systems. The reception area across from the Great Hall was restored to its 1896 appearance with refinishing of the original mahogany. The grand double staircases between the first and second floors were also restored. On the second floor, the Choate Room was increased in size. Librarians' offices were created on the third floor, as well as a new reading room with access to the fourth floor reading room by a nearby stairway. An office for the president of the Association was created on the fourth floor. A mezzanine floor with a new kitchen and dishwashing facility was also created above the basement. Rented space in the Bar Building would be used for the offices of the treasurer and to house a number of public interest functions.

The restoration began in August 1983. Most of the construction occurred while Louis Craco was president. He felt, he says, as if he were manager of a large construction project. Archibald Murray, who chaired the Executive Committee just prior to the restoration (1981–82), commented, "we were in the real estate and construction business for a while."[17]

Not surprisingly for a construction project, costs soared while the renovation was taking place, and it took longer than expected. The estimated construction budget had been $4.5 million; the total budget for the project, except for the restoration of existing marble and woods, had been $6.2 million. But the unexpected often occurs during construction. Two examples: walls were opened up and an aging electrical system found to be rotten; an air conditioning unit overflowed and ruined a freshly painted ceiling. In the end, the cost came to between $10 million and $11 million, of which $3 million went for refurbishment, new equipment, and a modern telephone system, and for such costs as the moving and cleaning of 500,000 books. Originally, it had been anticipated that the cost of renovation would be paid with the $4.2 million cash payment obtained through the sale of the Bar Building and the rest through borrowing—the interest and amortization to come from $10 million mortgage on the Bar Building. However, the $10 million mortgage note was disposed of in July 1986 for $9,975,000. The first $4.5 million of that was used to repay the indebtedness related to the restoration project and another $265,000 owed to the restoration consultant. This left $5 million for endowment. By June 1987, the treasurer could report on total Association assets of $18,950,000 and another $1,165,000 in the Association of the Bar of the City of New York Fund, and indebtedness of $781,000 for leases on library equipment. The Association's portfolio amounted to $8,342,000.

The first target for substantial completion of the project was early 1984, but substantial delays resulted from renovation of the second floor stairwell. Other delays were caused by the wiring problems. In October 1984 the new Whitney North Seymour Room on the east side of the lobby was dedicated. The House itself was rededicated on March 19, 1985, with the completion of the renovation of the marble staircase on the east side of the main entrance hall. That evening the Association Medal was awarded to Ruebhausen, Cyrus Vance, and Herbert Wechsler, while honorary membership was bestowed upon Justice Potter Stewart, Edward Weinfeld, Shirley Hufstedler, and Arthur Chaskalson, then director of the Legal Resources Center of Johannesburg and currently the president of the Constitutional Court of South Africa.[18]

COOPERATION WITH NEW YORK CITY'S
"LOCAL" BAR ASSOCIATIONS

Another major accomplishment of Oscar Ruebhausen's presidency was a substantial lessening of the historic tensions between the local bar associations and the City Bar and the beginnings of cooperation on matters of mutual concern. Throughout the first hundred years of the Association there had been differences in perspective between New York's "shirt sleeve lawyers" and its "parchment collar lawyers." The Association had been perceived as dominated by "parchment collar lawyers" and less than sensitive to the concerns of the smaller firms and individual practitioners, many of whom practiced in the "outer boroughs" (Brooklyn, Queens, The Bronx, and Staten Island). In Manhattan the New York County Lawyers' Association had come to be regarded as spokesman for the smaller practitioners. The screening of judicial candidates by the Association in the outer boroughs was particularly resented by lawyers (and politicians) from those boroughs, who were better attuned to what went on in their local courthouses than the Association was.[19] If it was an exaggeration to view the Association as "Brahmin dominated,"* it is fair to say that the perspectives of the outer boroughs during the first century had not been well represented in the Association.

Because Ruebhausen's involvements in the Association prior to his presidency had been with the "technical" scientific committees rather than its internal workings, he did not share the traditional wariness felt by leaders of the Association toward the local associations and was effective in creating opportunities for cooperation. Further, his self-perception as "a rebel against the establishment boys" added to his empathy for the perspectives of the local bar associations.[20]

At the time Ruebhausen became president, the county bars had the creation of a network of the smaller associations under consideration. When Ruebhausen invited the presidents of all the county bars to lunch, the presidents of the New York County Lawyers, the Richmond Bar, and the Queens Bar came, although the latter was not receptive to the overtures of the City Bar. Shortly thereafter, the president of the Brooklyn Bar Association invited Ruebhausen to a dinner which the president of the Bronx Bar also attended. That was followed by a dinner at Mario's restaurant in the Bronx. By then, real personal friendships were developing. Further links would be forged with the Puerto Rican Bar Association, the Harlem Bar, and the New York Women's Bar.

Cooperation on the issue most likely to cause friction between the City Bar and the local associations—evaluation of judicial nominees for the courts of the outer boroughs—was fostered by the efforts of

---

*To that charge, Paul De Witt once responded, "We have 10,000 members—by definition, they cannot all be Brahmins" (*New York Times*, October 1, 1982, p. 38).

the Association's Ed Costikyan. As early as the summer of 1981, Ruebhausen could report on new arrangements for the screening of judges in Manhattan, Brooklyn, and The Bronx. The qualifications of candidates were to be investigated by a joint subcommittee of representatives of the Association's Judiciary Committee and of the bar association from the county where the judgeship was. Candidates would be given just a single questionnaire and only one interview. However, each bar would then independently reach its own conclusions as to the candidates.[21]

During the remaining part of his tenure, Ruebhausen met frequently with the presidents of the local bars, especially Max Pfeiffer of The Bronx, Maurice Chayt of Brooklyn, and Harold Baer of the New York County Lawyers' Association. The Network of Bar Leaders was eventually formed during Ruebhausen's presidency as a coordinating body of the two dozen bar associations of New York City and Westchester including the City Bar. Louis Craco continued the personal relationships. By Robert McKay's presidency, the Network was meeting monthly and sponsoring a day-long program for legislators.[22] The Network would by Conrad Harper's presidency grow into an organization representing thirty-six county and specialty bar associations in the New York City metropolitan area, which lobbied as a unit with the state legislature for an agenda encompassing matters of judicial administration and substantive law.[23] It is an important example of how the Association during its fifth quarter-of-a-century has overcome its long heritage of lack of interest in cooperating with other organizations with common interests and common goals.*

VOLS

The most important achievement of Louis Craco's presidency was to stimulate an enormous expansion of *pro bono* work for the poor by the private bar through the creation in 1984 of Volunteers of Legal Service (VOLS). At its inception on May 1, 1984, twenty-nine large

*The dinners at Mario's have continued up to the present time.

law firms agreed to meet or exceed an annual goal of thirty hours of *pro bono* work per attorney.

There is nothing new about statements of concern by Association officers regarding the availability of legal services for the poor or about making some contribution to improving the situation. Support for The Legal Aid Society goes back generations. Support for an enhanced role by the City Bar grew during the 1960s after the Supreme Court recognized the right to counsel of every criminal defendant in felony prosecutions and Congress funded some civil legal services for the poor through the Criminal Justice and Economic Opportunity Acts of 1964. This heightened concern was represented by the highly unusual reprinting in the January 1965 *Record* of the seminal law review article written by Edgar S. and Jean C. Cahn which proposed neighborhood law firms.[24] The creation and growth of the Neighborhood Legal Services (NLS) program of the Office of Economic Opportunity was fostered the same year by the strong positive stand taken by the president of the American Bar Association that year, Lewis F. Powell, Jr., thus heading off possible attack by the organized bar of "socialized law practice."

The City Bar not only added its general support to the growth of the Neighborhood Legal Services program but, more practically, the Committee on Legal Assistance and the Committee on Professional Responsibility evaluated the petitions submitted to the Appellate Division for operation of the neighborhood law offices. Indeed, the "unremitting efforts" of George Brownell on behalf of the Association contributed to Appellate Division approval of Community Action for Legal Services to render such services in New York.[25]

When the Neighborhood Legal Services lawyers and the growing public interest bar broadened the scope of their activities from just litigation to lobbying, organizing community groups, and mobilizing demonstrations, there was a political reaction. The Nixon Administration threatened the independence of the OEO lawyers by supporting strong restrictions on the outside political activities of the staff attorneys of Neighborhood Legal Services. The City Bar supported the broadened role of lawyers for the poor. On February 28, 1973, for example, President Orville Schell testified before the House Subcommittee on Equal Opportunities on behalf of creation of an independent legal services corporation to protect the NLS lawyers from retaliation. He also urged emergency action to preserve the present OEO programs until the corporation had been established. "We believe," Schell said, "that the principle of professional independence means exactly the same thing for a lawyer who represents poor clients as it means for a lawyer who represents wealthy clients."[26] The effort to protect the independence of Neighborhood Legal Services lawyers was successful. In January 1975 an independent corporation for legal services was created, employing more than 2,000 attorneys. However, only a few years later, during the Reagan Administration, the Association again was rallying support (along with many other bar associations) for Neighborhood Legal Services, this time successfully fighting the attempt by the Reagan Administration to defund the organization.

New York Lawyers for the Public Interest

In the late 1960s, responding to pressures from associates and to the concerns of law students whom they were attempting to recruit, some of the large New York law firms began to provide legal services directly to nonpaying clients. However, in spite of these efforts and those of Neighborhood Legal Services and public interest law firms, as well as traditional *pro bono* programs, the needs remained great.

In 1976, Cyrus Vance and Adrian DeWind jointly announced the founding of New York Lawyers for the Public Interest, created by the Executive Committee of the Association to increase legal services to the poor through screening and channeling public law opportunities to participating large law firms. Joined in this venture were the Young Lawyers Committee and the Council of New York Law Associates. It was anticipated that in time the organization would do more than act as a clearing house, that it would provide legal services directly.

New York Lawyers for the Public Interest required those law firms and corporate law departments who joined to accept matters on referral and to make financial contributions to the organization. As its initial project, New York Lawyers for the Public Interest secured a major New York law firm to assist the city's Board of Correction in formulating minimum standards in the care and custody of individuals awaiting trials. The first executive director of New York Lawyers for the Public Interest was Daniel L. Kurtz, and the organization was located in the Bar Building.[27] By its fifteenth anniversary, which was celebrated on October 30, 1991, with a gala party, New York Lawyers for the Public Interest had sixty members—fifty-seven law firms and three corporate law departments. The scope of its work included matters of taxation, health care and health insurance, neighborhood preservation, land use planning, and corporate law.[28]

The Creation of VOLS

The next major step taken by the Association to facilitate legal services for the poor, the creation of VOLS, resulted from several factors, including the cuts made by the Reagan Administration in funding legal services for the poor, increasing professional acceptance of the view that representation by a lawyer in civil matters (in addition to criminal matters) was necessary to realize the ideal of equal justice under law, and the growing controversy over whether *pro bono* activities by lawyers should be mandated.*

Louis Craco saw the New York bar as a huge resource that needed mobilization. On May 1, 1984, Craco announced the formation of Volunteers of Legal Service (VOLS), a major initiative designed greatly to increase the amount of *pro bono* work by the private bar in the legal services area. Agreement had been reached with twenty-nine large law firms to provide at least thirty hours annually of *pro bono* work per attorney. "*Pro bono*" was essentially "limited" in this program to provision of legal services for the poor. The program had been organized by Sheldon Oliensis, chair of the Access to Legal Services Committee, who then became VOLS' first president (1984–

*In 1979, a Special Committee of the Association opposed such a requirement, viewing it as an ethical obligation which should not be enforced with disciplinary sanction. In 1981, the Executive Committee strongly endorsed *pro bono* service, but opposed any legal minimum and any requirement that *pro bono* service be reported. Later in the 1980s, after it became clear that the voluntary system had not been successful, a panel appointed by Chief Judge Sol Wachtler recommended that all lawyers in the state be required to donate at least twenty hours each year. The Association supported this proposal in principle—Sheldon Oliensis testifying before the Wachtler panel—but it has not been adopted.

86). Thomas H. Moreland, chair of the Committee on Legal Assistance, who had been in charge of formulating models for the use of volunteers, would become VOLS' second president. The effort to enlist the law firms had been headed by Cyrus Vance, and the recruitment of corporate law departments had been the charge of Richard S. Lombard, General Counsel of Exxon.

At the outset, VOLS focused on the areas of social security and unemployment claims, matrimonial and family law, landlord/tenant, immigration matters, and consumer law. New areas of emphasis and projects would emerge. VOLS also began to match law firms with the poverty law offices of Legal Services. Two law firms—LeBoeuf Lamb Greene & MacRae and Willkie Farr & Gallagher—each contributed the time of three associates for a year. In practice this meant twelve lawyers (in their second through fifth years) working four months each in a poverty law office. The associates from Willkie Farr, for example, worked at the Grand Street Office of Legal Services on the Lower East Side. Wachtell Lipton Rosen & Katz used a different approach. It provided, and still provides, funds for a fulltime attorney at MFY Legal Services. That office in 1984 had eight fulltime lawyers for an eligible population of 43,000, but, as a result of financial cutbacks, had but two in 1994. Patterson Belknap Webb & Tyler, Dewey Ballantine, Weil Gotshal & Manges, and Carter Ledyard & Milburn were among the other firms matched with poverty law offices.

From 1987 to 1989 VOLS operated a Legalization Support Project providing representation to undocumented aliens applying for legalized status under the 1986 Immigration Reform Act. That meant VOLS recruited and trained 350 volunteer lawyers to handle such matters as the representation of HIV-positive individuals who needed to establish that their presence in the United States did not constitute a danger to public health.

The VOLS AIDS Project, begun in 1988, assisted more than 2,000 clients in its first six years. Chaired by Alexander D. Forger, who later became president of the Legal Services Corporation, the project began at St. Clare's Hospital. Within six years it had expanded to eleven hospitals, four social service centers, two poverty law offices, a health clinic, and a subsidized housing complex, with a law firm matched with each project site. The lawyers in the VOLS AIDS Project help to prepare wills, living wills, and powers of attorney. They form part of a team, meeting as they do with physicians, nurses, and social workers in addition to the patients.

The VOLS Elderly Project, begun in 1991, now has 400 volunteer lawyers and works with 43 community-based social service agencies. Clients are matched directly with volunteer attorneys living in their neighborhood. Individual *pro bono* representation is provided, and legal clinics are conducted at local senior centers and in the community. Most of the matters dealt with involve wills and living wills, housing, social security, Medicare, Medicaid, and pensions. One very important further benefit for the clients is the lessening of their sense of isolation. As Francis X. Mahoney, a retired partner of Mudge Rose who staffs legal clinics on the Upper East Side, said, "[t]here are a lot of desperate, lonely people in New York City who, with a little bit of effort on a volunteer's part, can find their way through a lot of the struggles that overwhelm them."[29]

There is also a VOLS Children's Law Project, dealing with issues of education, entitlement, and health, in which Davis Polk & Wardwell participates with Advocates for Children and the Children's Defense Fund.

In 1993–94, participating law firms contributed a total of 423,418 hours of free legal services in a twelve-month period. Twenty-seven law firms had donated 30 to 120 hours per year per attorney *pro bono* time. Legal and technical assistance was provided by VOLS to more than 100 community-based organizations.[30] VOLS commemorated its tenth anniversary in 1994 at a dinner at which Chief Judge Judith S. Kaye of the New York Court of Appeals spoke.

CRIMINAL JUSTICE

In the 1970s, the Association had begun to make a major commitment to seek improvements in the criminal justice system and to try to improve the restoration of public confidence in that system. By 1981, seven separate committees with newly assigned functions had been organized to concentrate on different facets of criminal justice. Among the new committees were the Committee on Criminal Advocacy (chaired by William E. Hellerstein), Committee on Corrections (chaired by Bernard H. Goldstein), and the Committee on Criminal Law (chaired by Peter L. Zimroth). The work of each of the committees (save the Special Committee on Police Law and Policy) was coordinated by a Council on Criminal Justice, chaired first by Louis Craco and then by Robert McKay.

Spurred by Louis Craco, the council and seven committees organized in 1981 the first of a series of "retreats," each devoted to an aspect of criminal justice. All the major actors in the criminal justice system are brought together in these retreats and are joined by concerned lay persons. The subject of the first retreat was "Perspectives on the Judicial Functions in Criminal Justice." Among the nearly one hundred participants at the conference were Mayor Ed Koch, Court of Appeals judge Sol Wachtler, police, prosecutors, defense counsel, judges, media and civic groups.[31] The second retreat was devoted to selective incapacitation; the third, to the topic "The Criminal Justice System and the Public: Are They Communicating?"

THE WORK OF THE COMMITTEES

In 1982, a Subcommittee on Committee Service and Committee Structure, chaired by Robert Kaufman, delivered an important report to the Executive Committee on increasing the number of members who could participate in the work of the Association. The subcommittee rejected the ABA model of division into "sections" by substantive law issues, believing that unless section members are on a committee, they have little opportunity to make a contribution. The subcommittee also rejected both the creation of open committees and the recent proposal of the Special Committee on the Second Century for study groups to serve as adjuncts to existing committees. What the Subcommittee on Committee Service did recommend was that the size of *all* committees be increased to twenty-seven (then the upper limit), that new committees be established, and even that some committees should be divided on the basis of subject matter. The subcommittee also strongly supported diversity of opinions on committees, while strongly opposing the practice of members of committees sending a "delegate" from his/her law firm to represent him/her when absent and urged a much tougher policy on absences.[32]

The productivity and variety of the work of the committees did not diminish in the early 1980s, although it can only be hinted at here. The Committee on Federal Legislation considered pending legislation seeking to strip jurisdiction from the federal courts over school prayer, abortion, and school desegregation cases, concluding that they were "probably unconstitutional and certainly unwise."[33] The Committee on Consumer Affairs dealt with reforms in the funeral industry and with reform of Small Claims Court. The Committee on Legal Assistance continued to work to make legal services more widely available.[34] The Committee on Patents delivered a report on "Patent Protection for the Fruits of Genetic Engineering."[35] The Committee on Criminal Advocacy urged the Individual Calendar System on the New York City Criminal Court.[36] The Committee on Criminal Law thought it "unwise to modify or eliminate the Exclusionary Rule."[37] The Special Committee on the Lawyer's Role in Tax Practice considered a variety of ethical problems.[38] The Committee on Labor and Employment Law urged re-examination of the American rule, which permits the discharge at any time of at-will employees for any reason without their having legal recourse.[39] Other committees were dealing with the undercount of the census, the mandatory docket of the New York Court of Appeals, and extension of the Voting Rights Act.

NOTES

1. Interview with George Lindsay (see above, chap. 3, note 2).

2. *New York Times*, March 27, 1988.

3. *The Record*, 36 (November 1981), 449.

4. Interview with Archibald Murray (see above, chap. 2, note 56).

5. Interview with Robert MacCrate (see above chap. 2, note 2).

6. *44th Street Notes*, 7, No. 4 (April 1992), 1; *The Record*, 37 (January/February 1982), 1–2.

7. Oscar M. Ruebhausen, "Report of the President, *The Record*, 37 (October 1982), 528.

8. Interview with Louis Craco (see above, chap. 1, note 30).

9. Vance, "Acceptance of Honorary Membership" (see above, chap. 3, note 3), 15.

10. Robert M. Kaufman, "Second Inaugural Address," *The Record*, 42 (June 1987), 597.

11. *44th Street Notes*, 7, No. 4 (April 1992) 1, 2.

12. Interview with Sheldon Oliensis (see above, chap. 1, note 30).

13. Robert B. McKay, "Report of the President," *The Record*, 40 (October 1985), 425, 438–39.

14. *The Record*, 36 (November 1981), 447–48; Ruebhausen, "Report of the President" (see above, note 7), 512, 515, 524; *The Record*, 36 (December 1981), 553; Oscar M. Ruebhausen, "Report of the President," *The Record*, 36 (November 1981), 459ff.

15. Special Committee on the Second Century, "The Financial Affairs of the Association" (see above, chap. 1, note 39), 441.

16. Remarks of Robert McKay, "Stated Meeting and Rededication of the House," *The Record*, 40 (October 1985), 462, 463.

17. Interviews with Louis Craco (see above, chap. 1, note 30) and Archibald Murray (see above, chap. 2, note 56).

18. On the sale of the Bar Building and restoration of the House, see the special issue of *The Record: The Record*, 40, No. 5 (October 1985), 462–600; Oscar M. Ruebhausen, "The Restoration of the House," *The Record*, 38 (March 1983), 101ff.; Ruebhausen "Report of the President" (see above, note 7), 530–37; John G. McGoldrick, "Report of the Treasurer [May 1985]," *The Record*, 40 (October 1985), 457; John G. McGoldrick, "Report of the Treasurer [May 1986]," *The Record*, 41 (June 1986), 546; John G. McGoldrick, "Report of the Treasurer [November 1986]," *The Record*, 42 (January/February 1987), 13; John G. McGoldrick, "Report of the Treasurer [May 1987]," *The Record*, 42 (June 1987), 599ff.; Coleman T. Mobley, "Bar Renovates Its Home—But Not Without Cost," *American Lawyer*, March 10, 1986, p. 7.

19. Powell, *From Patrician to Professional Elite* (see above, chap. 1, note 2), pp. 221–22.

20. Interview with Oscar M, Ruebhausen (see above, chap. 1, note 3).

21. Oscar M. Ruebhausen, "Report of the President, 1980–1981," *The Record*, 36 (November 1981), 466–68. See also *The Record*, 36 (May/June 1981), 255–57; *The Record*, 36 (December 1981), 546–47; *The Record*, 37 (March 1982), 94.

22. Robert B. McKay, "Report of the President," *The Record*, 41 (December 1986), 870.

23. See, for example, "Network of Bar Leaders Targets State Legislators with Four-Point Program," *New York Law Journal*, March 16, 1992.

24. Edgar S. Cahn and Jean C. Cahn, "Implementing the Civilian Perspective—A Proposal for a Neighborhood Law Firm," *The Record*, 20 (January 1965), 1off. (reprinted from *Yale Law Journal* 73 [January 1964], 317).

25. Robert L. Patterson, Jr., "Legal Services to the Poor in a Period of Rising Expectations," *The Record*, 23 (November 1968), 556.

26. *The Record*, 28 (March 1973), 182, 184. See also *The Record*, 26 (January 1971), 3.

27. *The Record*, 31 (October 1976), 409–11; Powell, *From Patrician to Professional Elite* (see above, chap. 1, note 2), p. 162. See also Conrad K. Harper, "President's Column: The Association and the Fifteenth Anniversary of New York Lawyers for the Public Interest," *44th Street Notes*, 7, No. 1 (January 1992), 1–2.

28. Harper, "President's Column" (see above, note 27), 1, 2.

29. Abel, *American Lawyers* (see above, chap. 3, note 33), p. 133.

30. This section is based on the booklet "VOLS: Volunteers of Legal Service; 1984–1994—Ten Years of Service." See also "VOLS Marks 10 Years of Serving the Poor," *New York Law Journal*, October 14, 1994, p. 2.

31. Ruebhausen, "Report of the President" (see above, note 21), 459, 469–70.

32. "Report of the Subcommittee on Committee Service and Committee Structure," *The Record*, 37 (December 1982), 687.

33. Committee on Federal Legislation, "Jurisdiction Stripping Proposals in Congress: The Threat to Judicial Constitutional Review," *The Record*, 36 (December 1981), 557.

34. Association of the Bar of the City of New York, Minutes of the Stated Meeting, November 18, 1980, pp. 59–61.

35. *The Record*, 37 (May 1982), 368.

36. Committee on Criminal Advocacy, "The Individual Calendar System—A Needed Reform for the New York City Criminal Court," *The Record*, 37 (May 1982), 301.

37. Committee on Criminal Law, "Report on the Exclusionary Rule," *The Record*, 37 (November 1982), 598.

38. "Ethics and the Tax Lawyer," *The Record*, 38 (April 1983), 218.

39. "At-Will Employment and the Problem of Unjust Dismissal," *The Record*, 36 (May/June, 1981), 170.

6

"We Saved Roe Against Wade": The Association of the Bar, 1984–88

ALTHOUGH DURING THE YEARS 1984–88 there were important developments within the Association respecting diversity and toward greater direct involvement in the delivery of legal services for the poor (both considered in the following chapter), the central event was the Association's stand against the confirmation of Judge Robert Bork as Justice of the Supreme Court of the United States.

THE PRESIDENTS: ROBERT McKAY AND ROBERT KAUFMAN

Surely Robert McKay was one of the most beloved presidents in the Association's history. Born in Wichita on August 1, 1919, the son of a ship's blacksmith who had gone into the grain business, McKay earned a bachelor's degree from the University of Kansas and his law degree from Yale. Joining the army three months before the Second World War began, McKay was a captain at war's end. For three years he served as an attorney with the Department of Justice (1947–50) before turning to the academic world. McKay taught at Emory Law School (1950–53) before moving to the New York University School of Law, which he never left. As a scholar, he was best known for his work in the area of legislative reapportionment. As the highly popular dean of NYU Law School during tumultuous times (1967–75), McKay promoted clinical legal studies and fostered the study of legal ethics. The prestige of the law school rose greatly during his tenure.

McKay's work with the City Bar—for whom he chaired the Executive Committee, Nominating Committee, and the Council on Criminal Justice, in addition to being active in the criminal justice retreats—was just a small part of his professional activities. McKay chaired the board of the New York Civil Liberties Union and the Citizens Union and was president of Legal Aid. He chaired a number of ABA bodies, including the committee that recommended mandatory continuing legal education for lawyers and the committee that studied the adequacy of lawyer discipline. He was Senior Fellow of the Aspen Institute for Humanistic Studies and director of its program on Justice, Society, and the Individual. McKay worked toward increasing opportunities for women and minorities in the legal profession, promoted public interest law, advocated expanded *pro bono* efforts, and supported increased funding of the federal legal services program. Perhaps his most important public service came as chairman of the New York State Special Commission on the Attica prison riot, the bloodiest in U.S. prison history. The "McKay Commission" was sharply critical of state prison authorities and Governor Nelson Rockefeller. After his presidency, McKay remained active in the Association, making international human rights missions and serving as chair of the Special Committee on the Second Century. As John Feerick saw it, McKay left his "imprint in every area of the legal profession—in the aggregate, more than any other lawyer I have known or probably ever will know."

Robert McKay died on July 13, 1990. He is remembered by his City Bar colleagues as "fairness incarnate," "a man who spoke in paragraphs," a "gentle man who never spoke ill of anyone, but [also] a man of basic integrity and strength." He had, to paraphrase another colleague's comment, the capacity to pull together the strands and threads of the thinking of others and synthesize with intellectual agility and eloquence. His greatest strength, a colleague said, was his ability to come up with a "completely inclusive solution." "Everyone was touched by his goodness," John Feerick said," and Conrad Harper commented that, "there was nothing of the stentorian about him, no noise, merely the serenity of a great man doing great work."[1]

Robert Kaufman was the second president of the Association to be born abroad (the first was John G. Milburn, born in England, and president 1919–20). After his parents fled from Vienna via England, Kaufman came to America at the age of ten. He attended Bronx High School of Science; Brooklyn College, where he also earned a graduate degree in economics; and Brooklyn Law School at night. Kaufman got his first job as a lawyer as a result of his participation in the Association's moot court competition. He was spotted in the competition by the head of the New York Office of the Antitrust Division of the Department of Justice. Kaufman next worked for Senator Jacob Javits of New York, where part of his duties was to act as liaison with the Association's Committee on Federal Legislation. Kaufman later joined the firm of Proskauer Rose Goetz & Mendelsohn, where he became a partner. A transactional lawyer, he specialized in health and hospital law as well as multinational corporate law, demonstrating a great understanding of financial markets. He served on the Association's Committee on Federal Legislation and its Committee on Congressional Ethics, before being named chairman by Francis Plimpton of the Committee on Civil Rights. Kaufman was also chair of the Committee on Professional Responsibility and of both the Special Committee on the Second Century and the Executive Committee (during Oscar Ruebhausen's presidency). He has also served on the Board of The Legal Aid Society, was a member of the Board of Visitors of the U.S. Military Academy, and is a trustee of Brooklyn Law School. Kaufman has also chaired the Committee on Regulation of the Administrative Conference of the United States and the Fund for Modern Courts.

Kaufman has been described as "a caring man without a discriminatory bone in his body, who could get along with anyone," "a visionary," and "a reformer with political savvy." In 1995 Kaufman received the Association Medal, only the fifteenth person so honored since the Medal was established in 1951.[2]

Robert Kaufman's goals as president were to focus attention on the relationship between the public and the law and on the courts the public sees most—Housing, Family, Small Claims, and Criminal. As president, he undertook a series of visits to those courts to focus attention on their needs.[3] He was also interested in the tort system, juvenile justice, and the treatment of women in the courts. Indeed, Kaufman would be honored by the New York Women's Bar for his efforts on behalf of the inclusion of women—in the Association and in his firm—at the same time as Fern Schair was similarly honored. As president, Kaufman spurred membership growth and helped improve the City Bar's financial position. Two of his major achievements as president—his contributions to greater diversity within the profession and the beginnings of the Association's direct provision of legal services to those in need—are addressed in the following chapter. Nevertheless, his presidency will undoubtedly be remembered most for the Association's stand on Robert Bork's nomination to the Supreme Court.

THE ASSOCIATION AND THE BORK NOMINATION

Ronald Reagan's nomination of Robert Bork to the Supreme Court of the United States in the summer of 1987 brought about one of the great constitutional debates in modern times and the most substantive debate in American history over the constitutional views of a court nominee. The Association contributed to that debate and to the defeat of Bork.

The stakes appeared to be extremely high in the fight over the confirmation of Judge Bork. Ronald Reagan had signaled early in his first term that he intended to dramatically change the direction of the High Court. But his three appointments in his first six and a half years—Sandra Day O'Connor (replacing Potter Stewart), William Rehnquist (elevated to replace Warren Burger as Chief Justice), and Antonin Scalia (to Rehnquist's seat)—had not changed the orientation of the High Court much. However, the appointment of Bork to replace Lewis F. Powell, Jr. (the Court's balance wheel in many of its major cases between 1972 and 1986) appeared to presage a major swing. Further, there was most probably more at stake than simply the switch of a vote from moderately "conservative" to decidedly "conservative" or the creation of a five-person majority. Intellectually formidable and possessing a well-thought-out judicial philosophy, Bork seemed equipped to emerge as the leader of a "new court." Finally, the appointment of Judge Bork seemed to place in great jeopardy *Roe v. Wade*, the most controversial decision of the era, in which the Supreme Court had held that a woman's right to choose whether to have or not to have a child was a constitutional right entitled to at least qualified protection.

Although Bork was superbly equipped for the Court intellectually, his confirmation was no sure thing. The Democratic Party controlled the Senate. The Reagan Administration was distracted and weakened by the Iran–Contra Affair. Then, too, Bork brought baggage of his own to the confirmation struggle. Proselytizing for his judicial views for years—some argued that he had been barnstorming for the Supreme Court appointment—Bork had made no secret of his jurisprudential views, including his sharp criticism of the Court's opinion in *Roe v. Wade*. Furthermore, as a young lawyer, Bork had opposed on constitutional grounds the Public Accommodations section of what became the Civil Rights Act of 1964. As a more mature lawyer (and Acting Attorney General), Bork had wielded the knife for Richard Nixon that had struck down Archibald Cox.

The only time the City Bar had ever opposed a nominee to the Supreme Court of the United States who was neither a New Yorker nor a member of New York Bar was with the nomination of G. Harold Carswell. However, just two years before Bork was nominated, the Special Committee on the Second Century, then chaired by Robert McKay, had recommended that the Association add to the judicial nominees it examined nominees to the U.S. Court of Appeals for the Second Circuit from Connecticut and Vermont, bankruptcy judges in the Southern and Eastern Districts of New York, a number of state judges (including appointees to the Appellate Division), nominees to the U.S. Court of Appeals for the District of Columbia Circuit, *and* appointments to the U.S. Supreme Court. The committee had argued that "the substantial impact that a Supreme Court Justice can have on the evolution of federal law makes review by the Association desirable"; that since the Association often "made known its views on issues that affect the nation as a whole," surely "[t]he quality of a Supreme Court nominee is in general a far more significant matter of public concern than the outcome of a case before the Court or the quality of a piece of federal legislation."[4] Responsibility for evaluation of U.S. Supreme Court nominees was vested in the Executive Committee, which adopted the new policy at its meeting of May 6, 1987, a few weeks before Powell's retirement was announced.

Treading in new waters, Joan L. Ellenbogen, chair of the Executive Committee, after consulting with Kaufman, appointed Sheila L. Birnbaum, a vice president of the Association, to chair a nine-person ad hoc committee on the Bork nomination. Four additional members of the Executive Committee and four members of the Judiciary Committee were also appointed. That ad hoc committee read all Bork's judicial opinions and articles and interviewed more than thirty-five judges, law professors, and former colleagues. (Understandably, Bork, who made himself available for lengthy questioning by the Senate Judiciary Committee, did not consent to be interviewed by the Association committee.)

After the ad hoc committee reported to the Executive Committee, the latter, aware that it was setting a precedent, debated its position at considerable length. But, as Robert Kaufman later described it, "because the man stood against everything the Association stood for," the Executive Committee voted 17 to 4 to disapprove the nomination.[5]

On September 11, four days before the Senate Judiciary Committee hearings on Bork began, the Executive Committee announced its opposition to him. It stated that "[w]hile the qualities of Judge Bork's intellect and professional experience [are] not in dispute, this cannot be the end of the inquiry for the Association or the Senate of the United States." The Senate, "in addition to considering the professional competence of a candidate, has both a right and a constitutional duty to consider the judicial and constitutional philosophy of a nominee to the Supreme Court." As to that, the committee held: "Judge Bork's fundamental judicial philosophy, as expressed repeatedly and consistently over the past thirty years in his writings, public statements and judicial decisions appears to this Association to run counter to many of the fundamental rights and liberties protected by the Constitution."[6]

The City Bar was the first organization whose reason for being was unlinked to specific value positions to announce its opposition to Judge Bork. In contrast, the American Bar Association Committee on the Federal Judiciary divided over Bork—ten members giving him the highest recommendation, four finding him "not qualified," and one stating that he was "not opposed." On September 25, Kaufman and Birnbaum appeared before the Senate Judiciary Committee. Kaufman read the statement agreed upon by the Executive Committee, which concluded that a majority of members of the Executive Committee was "convinced" that the appointment of Bork "would detrimentally affect the rights of individuals and groups that the Supreme Court has recognized and protected, and that access to the courts may be seriously curtailed."[7] That day, three former ABA presidents testified on behalf of Bork (while five others had endorsed him), but two others, Robert Meserve and Chesterfield Smith, joined Kaufman in opposition.

The City Bar's stand angered some of its members (it still angers some of its members!). Fifty-three, including five sitting judges, immediately signed a letter of protest, arguing that the Executive Committee's conduct had been unauthorized, irregular, and political.[8] Paul J. Curran, a partner in Kaye Scholer and a former U.S. Attorney, resigned from the Association over the issue, and it appears that possibly another twenty-five members did as well. In December, there was another statement in opposition, signed by one hundred members. In contrast, more than two hundred communications supported the Association's position. Furthermore, an enormous increase in the membership of the Association occurred during the year.*

What, then, may have been achieved by the Association's wading into these political waters? Harvey Goldschmid, Columbia University law professor and chair of the Executive Committee in the year 1984–85, says that what the Association did was to make opposition to Bork "mainstream," adding credibility to the opposition to him.[9] Was more than that achieved? In San Francisco early in the morning of June 29, 1992, Robert Kaufman, seeing a copy of *The New York Times*, read that the Supreme Court had decided *Planned Parenthood of Southeastern Pennsylvania v. Casey*, the case it was expected the High Court would use as a vehicle to overturn *Roe v. Wade*. The High Court had not done what was expected. *Roe* had survived, the result of a remarkable opinion written jointly by Justices Sandra Day O'Connor, Anthony Kennedy (who ultimately filled the Powell vacancy on the Court), and David Souter. When Kaufman caught his breath, he telephoned Fern Schair in New York and said to her, "We saved Roe against Wade."[10] An overstatement? Perhaps. But, it ought

*But not necessarily because of the opposition to Bork.

to be remembered, at least part of the reason *Roe's* author, Harry Blackmun, was on the Supreme Court, was that Carswell had not been confirmed, and at least part of the reason Anthony Kennedy was on the Court was that Bork had not been confirmed. Thus, the Association had at least made contributions to the spawning of *Roe* and to its salvation.

In early January 1988, when the Executive Committee was about to make a recommendation on the nomination of Anthony Kennedy to the Supreme Court,* several members of the Association sought a restraining order from state Supreme Court. Kaufman found out about the lawsuit during the afternoon of January 4, two days before the Executive Committee was supposed to meet. Papers were served on the evening of the 4th, and the hearing on the order to show cause took place the following day. Kaufman, Joan Ellenbogen, and Sheila Birnbaum appeared before Judge Edward J. Greenfield to defend the Association on a cold January day.

The dissident members contended in [Winthrop J.] *Allegaert v.* [Robert M.] *Kaufman* that evaluations of U.S. Supreme Court justices were "illegal, unauthorized and *ultra vires*" because no provision of the Association's constitution or bylaws conferred such power or authority upon the Executive Committee.[11] Early in the hearing on January 5th, Judge Greenfield, with whom the Association had clashed sometime before over the issue of court unification, asked Richard Nolan, who was arguing *pro se*:

> But what is there to restrict the Executive Committee from issuing a pronouncement on any subject, the lack of due process in Soviet trials, for example, or alleged maltreatment of Palestinians in Israel or I seem to recall an instance where the President of the Bar Association and the Executive Committee endorsed a lawyer's march in opposition to the Vietnam War.[12]

Greenfield went to the nub of the case early by pointing to Article 8, Section II of the Association's constitution—its "elastic clause," which reads:

---

*Douglas Ginsburg, President Reagan's second nominee for the Powell vacancy, asked to have his name withdrawn after accusations that he publicly smoked marijuana while he was a faculty member of the Harvard Law School. This withdrawal occurred before any Association evaluation.

"In addition to such powers as are specifically conferred upon it by the constitution or other bylaw, the general management of the affairs of the Association shall be subject to the direction of the Executive Committee."[13]

In his argument, Kaufman pointed out that in the act of incorporation of the Association it states: "One of the purposes of the Association is facilitating the administration of justice." He went on: "There is nothing, frankly, in my view, which is more important to the administration of justice than the process of selection of judges who administer justice."[14] To which Judge Greenfield replied: "It doesn't say facilitating the administration of justice in New York State."[15]

Judge Greenfield denied the temporary restraining order. On the 6th, the Executive Committee voted to inform the membership that it had evaluated Kennedy positively, but delayed dissemination of that information until the afternoon of January 8th.[16] The plaintiffs then withdrew their motion as moot.

The Bork imbroglio may have impacted on the Association's tax status. The City Bar is qualified as a tax-exempt organization under Section 501 (c) (6) of the Internal Revenue Code. This renders it exempt from income tax. In 1982 the Association also applied for status under Section 501 (c) (3). Such 501 (c) (3) status would have made the Association eligible for exemption from the sales tax on books and other library material, perhaps a savings on real estate taxes, and eligibility for lower bulk-mailing postal rates. To qualify for 501 (c) (3) status, an organization not only must operate for charitable and educational purposes, but also must not "participate in, or intervene in (including the publishing or distributing of statements) any political campaign on behalf of (or in opposition to) any candidate for public office."

The IRS denied the request, taking the position that because the Association rates candidates running for judicial office, it was an "action" organization which participates in political activities and, therefore, barred from 501 (c) (3) status. If the Association chooses to give up evaluating elected judges, it would be entitled to receive 501 (c) (3) status. The Association brought an action in the Tax Court which it won by a vote of 10 to 6. The IRS appealed to the U.S. Court of

Appeals for the Second Circuit, where M. Bernard Aidinoff of Sullivan & Cromwell, who had long advised the Association on tax matters (and chaired the Executive Committee in 1977–78), argued for the Association.

Aidinoff called the oral argument "a disaster," for the Bork evaluation was referred to constantly.[17] The panel of Ellsworth A. Van Graafeiland, J. Daniel Mahoney, and Charles M. Metzner unanimously ruled against the Association. Writing for the court, Judge Van Graafeiland stated that one of the Association's most significant activities was rating candidates for both appointive and elective judgeships. To the argument that the Association's evaluation was "non-partisan," the court noted that: "A candidate who receives a 'not qualified' rating will derive little comfort from the fact that the rating may have been made in a nonpartisan manner." The Court of Appeals also rejected the contention that what the Association was putting forward was "objective data." "Ratings, by their very nature," the court said, "necessarily will reflect the philosophy of the organization conducting such activities."[18] That decision in *Association of the Bar of the City of New York v. Commissioner of Internal Revenue* may cost the Association as much as $100,000 per year.

Kennedy and Souter

For all nominees to the Supreme Court of the United States since Robert Bork, with the exception of the ill-fated Douglas Ginsburg, the Association has employed the same methods of evaluation: A subcommittee of the Executive Committee has been appointed to read the opinions of the nominee and interview his/her colleagues and then report to the full Executive Committee.

The Executive Committee was unanimous in recommending that Anthony Kennedy be approved.[19] It was more reserved about the nomination of David H. Souter. Though it found him "thoughtful, fair, diligent and independent," the Committee noted its concerns "flowing from his limited experience in dealing with the important and sensitive areas of constitutional law that come before the United States Supreme Court, and from several of his statements on these issues." Although the committee said it might want "to revisit the issues," it rated Souter "qualified" and did not make a return visit.[20]

Shortly after the Souter nomination, the Executive Committee in November 1990 codified guidelines for its evaluation of nominees to the United States Supreme Court. The guidelines read:

> In evaluating all nominees to the Supreme Court of the United States, pursuant to the Executive Committee resolution of May 7, 1987, the Executive Committee should be guided by its findings, based on the available evidence, on the extent to which a nominee possesses the following qualifications: exceptional legal ability; extensive experience and knowledge of the law; outstanding intellectual and analytical talents; maturity of judgment; unquestionable integrity and independence; a temperament reflecting a willingness to search for a fair resolution of each case before the Court; a sympathetic understanding of the Court's role under the Constitution in the protection of the personal rights of individuals; and an appreciation for the historic role of the Supreme Court as the final arbiter of the meaning of the United States Constitution, including a sensitivity to the respective powers and reciprocal responsibilities of the Congress and the Executive.[21]

Battle with the Bush Administration

In 1991, the Department of Justice told judicial nominees not to cooperate with the City Bar in its investigation and evaluation of their fitness for office and warned candidates for nominations that they would not be put forward if they agreed to evaluation by the Association. On April 15, 1991, Murray Dickman, a top aide to Attorney General Dick Thornburg, wrote to the Association, stating peremptorily: "Your interference in the constitutional process of selecting and appointing federal judges must end." The explicit reason given by the Justice Department was that, as it had agreed to work with the American Bar Association, it could not "let everybody get their nose under the tent." It must have been the Bork affair that stuck in the craw of the Bush Administration, for the Association had objected to only two of the forty-four nominees for federal judgeships it had evaluated between 1976 and 1991 (Thomas J. Meskill and Robert Bork). In addition, the ABA in 1989 had informed the Justice Department that it would *not* consider ideology in evaluating judicial appointments.

The Association battled back. Conrad Harper, then president of the Association, wrote in *The Washington Post* that "[t]he Justice Department's policy is intended to be and is in fact one of intimidation of nominees and local bar associations."[22] Four distinguished judges of the Court of Appeals for the Second Circuit, two appointed by Republican Presidents and two by Democratic Presidents—J. Edward Lumbard, Irving R. Kaufman, Wilfred Feinberg, and James L. Oakes—protested, writing to the Justice Department that "refusing to consider the city bar is an invitation to mediocrity or worse." The four judges also stated that they were disturbed by the First Amendment implications of the Department of Justice's informing potential appointees to the federal courts that, if they even interview with a committee from their local bar association, they would no longer be considered for a federal judgeship.[23] In *The New York Times*, former Judge Marvin E. Frankel thundered: "What meat do these Caesars feed on, and what strange Constitution do they read, to conclude that they may *order* the City Bar not to inquire and the candidates not to respond?"[24] To the Justice Department's suggestion that the City Bar should send its views to the American Bar Association, Harper answered that the City Bar did not work for the ABA.

The affair ended not with a bang, but with a whimper, when, in the spring of 1992, Harper quietly informed the membership that the dispute with the Justice Department was over and that the Association had evaluated all six of the then current nominees to the Southern and Eastern Districts of New York and to the Court of Appeals for the Second Circuit.[25]

Thomas, Ginsburg, and Breyer

When Clarence Thomas was appointed to the Supreme Court, the Executive Committee invited the membership of the Association to a forum (and/or to provide views in writing) before it issued its evaluation of Thomas. The forum on Thomas seems to have been "relatively calm."[26] However, in its evaluation of Thomas, the Executive Committee does not seem to have held the nominee to the standards of its guidelines of November 1990. Over the strong opposition of then Association president Conrad Harper, himself African-American, the Association issued a statement which can generously be characterized as "wishy-washy." The statement said that Thomas met "to a sufficient degree, those aspects of the Association's guidelines that pertain to legal ability, experience and knowledge in law, intellect, judgment, integrity, independence and temperament." That Thomas had "exceptional legal ability" was doubtful. That Thomas lacked "extensive experience and knowledge of the law," "outstanding intellectual and analytical talents," and "maturity of judgment" was patent. The Executive Committee did, however, state that "it had been unable to reach an overall judgment because of the nature of Judge Thomas' public statements bearing upon . . . whether Judge Thomas has a sympathetic understanding of the Court's role under the Constitution in the protection of the personal rights of individuals." The Executive Committee, therefore, urged that the Senate make "a thorough inquiry of Judge Thomas concerning his views in this area of fundamental importance" and take account of the full range of Thomas' constitutional philosophy in deciding whether to confirm.[27]

With the vastly better-qualified Ruth Bader Ginsburg, who as a law professor had been involved with the Association (as had her husband, Martin Ginsburg), there was no need to mince words. After the subcommittee, chaired by Allan Gropper and Helaine Barnett, reported, the Executive Committee endorsed its finding that Ginsburg "possesses to a *substantial degree* all of the qualifications enumerated in the Association's Guidelines." President John Feerick testified before the Senate Judiciary Committee in support of the nominee.[28]

The Association also found Stephen G. Breyer "qualified" after looking in particular into cases upon which he as a First Circuit judge had decided involving "Superfund" environmental liability under federal law, rather than having recused himself because of his investments in Lloyd's of London syndicates and thus his possible personal liability for underwriting losses. President Barbara Paul Robinson testified on Breyer's behalf.[29]

SOUTH AFRICA

Association policy toward South Africa was another difficult issue that the Association dealt with in the McKay–Kaufman period. After years of pressures, discussions, missions, the election of Arthur Chaskalson, director of the Legal Resources Centre of Johannesburg, to honorary membership, and the hosting of Bishop Desmond Tutu, the Executive Committee finally adopted a policy statement on South Africa. On the basic premise of racial superiority which undergirded the South African government, the Association stated:

> Such a philosophical outlook is not unprecedented, but South Africa appears to stand alone in the post–World War II era, if not in the degree of its brutality, then at least in the publicly expressed, officially enforced and legally sanctioned underpinnings of its system of racial subjugation.[30]

The announced goal of the Association was to foster substantive justice and procedural due process in South Africa. The policy statement emphasized that the Association's basic involvement with South African issues should be on a programmatic basis: "review by committees of appropriate subjects relating to United States–South African matters." At the same time, the Association also implemented divestiture of most of its investments in companies doing business with South Africa and undertook the monitoring of the effectiveness of U.S. economic sanctions.[31]

COMMITTEES

During the presidencies of Robert McKay and Robert Kaufman, a Council on International Affairs was created, a Special Committee on the Legal Problems of the Mentally Ill, as well as committees on International Trade, the Legal Problems of the Aging, and Tort Litigation. At the request of Mayor Edward Koch, two committees were created—one to study the state's election law and "its highly technical restrictions on access to the ballot" and another to deal with the problem of the amenities that communities demanded of those siting projects in New York City.

During these years, there were reports on "Drug Testing in the Workplace" by both the Committee on Labor and Employment Law and the Committee on Civil Rights.[32] The Committee on Federal Legislation reported on "The Line-Item Veto" and subjected to analysis the thirty-two state resolutions and memorials calling for a constitutional convention to propose a Balanced Budget Amendment to determine whether they were valid applications within the meaning of Article V of the U.S. Constitution.[33] The Committee on Communications Law, reporting on "Punitive Damages in Libel Actions," concluded that the trend toward "huge, arbitrary awards of punitive damages, whether or not sustained on appeal, have inhibited and continues to inhibit significantly the full, robust free speech envisioned under the First Amendment, to the detriment of our society." The committee called for the abolition of punitive damages in libel actions.[34] The Committee on Criminal Advocacy strongly disapproved of the forfeiture provisions of the Comprehensive Crime Control Act of 1984 and urged substantial substantive modifications to limit its reach, except when attorneys' fees are clearly a fraud and sham transaction.[35]

Two of the more important reports of the period dealt with AIDS. The Committee on Medicine and Law, chaired by Beatrice S. Frank, reported on a proposal of the New York City Department of Health to change the law to permit non-prescription purchases of hypodermic needles. The purpose of legalizing the sale of hypodermic needles was to reduce the spread of the AIDS virus among the second largest risk group, intravenous drug users, of which there were then 200,000 in New York City. Those opposing the change, including the district attorneys of all five boroughs, argued, in part, that needle sharing among users is ingrained social behavior and therefore that legalization would not help curb the spread of AIDS. The committee, however, supported the proposal, arguing that a fatal disease "should not be used as a deterrent for drug abuse" and held that the available evidence supported the conclusion that a significant percentage of drug users would seek to avoid contracting AIDS by using clean needles, were such needles readily available to them.[36]

The Joint Subcommittee on AIDS in the Criminal Justice System (of the Committee on Corrections and the Criminal Justice Operations and Budget Committee) rendered its first report in 1987.[37] It was sobering. The report began by noting that the majority of AIDS cases in the nation's prisons and jails had occurred in New York, New Jersey, and Pennsylvania (the result of the great number of intravenous drug users in the New York metropolitan area). Indeed, AIDS had become the leading cause of death in New York State correctional facilities. The subcommittee looked to the future and saw that "everything that is known about AIDS and the populations it most affects suggests that the criminal justice system in New York will find, not hundreds, but many thousands of persons with AIDS and related conditions in its midst by the end of this decade." Since no cure or vaccine for AIDS exists, the criminal justice system would have to prepare to deal with the "catastrophic problems that those numbers bode."[38] Not the least of the problems would be those confronted by a sentencing judge, who would know that with some defendants even a relatively short sentence might be tantamount to a life sentence, while, on the other hand, a light sentence could put at risk of AIDS those outside the prison. The committee also considered the problem of mass-screening in the absence of adequate counseling and education and the very troubling prospect of segregating or attempting to segregate prisoners with AIDS.

Two years later, the Joint Subcommittee delivered a 241-page report sharply criticizing the handling of AIDS by the criminal justice systems of state and city.[39] The report estimated that some 7,000 of the state's 44,000 prisoners might be HIV-positive, and that in New York City 10,000 to 15,000 of the 100,000 inmates who passed through the system in 1988 were HIV-positive. Not only were there problems of coordination, planning, inconsistent practices, and inadequate resources in dealing with AIDS, but defendants with the disease had been denied access to counsel and courtroom and had been treated like untouchables.[40]

NOTES

1. Based on interviews with George G. Gallantz (see above, chap. 1, note 3); Harvey Goldschmid (see above, chap. 2, note 60); Conrad Harper (see above, chap.

3, note 1); William Hellerstein (see above, chap. 2. note 56); Robert MacCrate (see above, chap. 5, note 5). See also Robert B. McKay, *44th Street Notes* 5, No. 6 (September 1990), 1; *New York Times*, July 10, 1990. See also "Topics of the Times: A Lawyer to Trust," *New York Times*, July 18, 1990, p. A20; [Robert M. Kaufman], "Presentation of McKay Portrait to the Association, May 24, 1988," *The Record*, 43 (October 1988), 646ff. And see "Memorial for Robert McKay, 1919–1990— President of the Association, 1984–1986," *The Record*, 45 (December 1990), 911–23.

2. Interviews with William Hellerstein (see above, chap. 2, note 56); Sheldon Oliensis (see above, chap. 1, note 31); George Gallantz (see above, chap. 1, note 3); Joan Ellenbogen, March 10, 1995; Thomas H. Moreland, March 2, 1995. See also *44th Street Notes*, 2, Nos. 4 (April 1987) and 5 (October 1986).

3. Robert M. Kaufman, "Second Inaugural Address" (see above, chap. 5, note 10), 594. See also *44th Street Notes*, 1, No. 8 (December 1986), 1–2.

4. Special Committee on the Second Century, "Association Review of Individuals Being Considered for Positions of Public Trust: An Executive Committee Position," *The Record*, 42 (October 1987), 788.

5. Interview with Robert M. Kaufman (see above, chap. 2, note 56). See also Robert M. Kaufman, "Letter from the President," *44th Street Notes*, 2, No. 11 (December 1987), 1.

6. Unpublished Statement by the Association of the Bar of the City of New York Issued by the Executive Committee 9/11/87 [sic]. See also Press Release, "The Association of the Bar of the City of New York Opposes Appointment of Judge Robert Bork" (on file with Association library).

7. Unpublished Statement of Robert M. Kaufman on the Nomination of Robert Bork (on file in Association library).

8. *New York Post*, September 25, 1987.

9. Interview with Harvey Goldschmid (see above, chap. 2, note 60).

10. Related to the author by Robert Kaufman.

11. Affidavit of Richard E. Nolan filed with Order to Show Cause in *Allegaert v. Kaufman*, Index No. 3/88.

12. Transcript of hearing in *Allegaert v. Kaufman*, p. 13 (copy on file in Association library).

13. Ibid., pp. 12–13.

14. Ibid., p. 29.

15. Ibid.

16. Letter from Robert M. Kaufman to Hon. Edward J. Greenfield, January 7, 1988 (unpublished copy on file in Association library).

17. Interview with M. Bernard Aidinoff (see above, chap. 1, note 3).

18. *Association of the Bar of the City of New York v. Commissioner*, No. 88-400l, pp. 9, 10.

19. Unpublished News Release [of Association of the Bar of the City of New York], 1/8/88, "The Association of the Bar of the City of New York Approves Appointment of Judge Anthony M. Kennedy" (copy on file in Association library).

20. *The Record*, 45 (October 1990), 690.

21. *The Record*, 45 (November 1990), 828.

22. Conrad Harper, "Justice Department Intimidation," *Washington Post*, August 19, 1991, p. A17, reprinted in *44th Street Notes*, 6, No. 9 (November 1991), 1, 2.

23. *Washington Post*, June 4, 1991; *New York Times*, June 4, 1991; Conrad K.

Harper and Fern Sussman, "Don't Bar Our Local Bar," *New York Newsday*, June 18, 1991.

24. Marvin E. Frankel, "Caesars at the Justice Department," *New York Times*, June 18, 1991.

25. Conrad K. Harper, "Farewell Address," *The Record*, 47 (October 1992), 585, 587; interview with Conrad K. Harper (see above, chap. 3, note 1).

26. Interview with Conrad K. Harper (see above, chap. 3, note 1).

27. "Statement of the Association of the Bar of the City of New York Issued by the Executive Committee," September 6, 1991 (on file in Association library).

28. *The Record*, 48 (October 1993), 669; interview with Merrell E. Clark (see above, chap. 2, note 8).

29. Statement, "The Association of the Bar of the City of New York Finds Judge Stephen G. Breyer Qualified to Be Justice of the Supreme Court," Unpublished News Release of July 8, 1994 (on file in Association library).

30. "The Association's Policy on South African Matters: An Executive Committee Statement," *The Record*, 42 (May 1987), 423.

31. See Robert M. Kaufman, "Report of the President, 1986–87," *The Record*, 42 (October 1987), 744, 748–49.

32. The report of the Committee and Employment Law is found in *The Record*, 43 (May 1988), 447; that of the Committee on Civil Rights in *The Record*, 43 (May 1988), 401.

33. *The Record*, 41 (April 1986), 307; Committee on Federal Legislation, "An Analysis of State Resolutions Calling for a Constitutional Convention to Propose a Balanced Budget Amendment," *The Record*, 40 (December 1985), 710.

34. *The Record*, 42 (January/February 1987), 20, 47.

35. "The Forfeiture of Attorneys Fees in Criminal Cases: A Call for Immediate Remedial Action," *The Record*, 41 (May 1986), 469, 511.

36. Committee on Medicine and Law, "Legalization of Non-Prescription Sale of Hypodermic Needles: A Response to the AIDS Crisis," *The Record*, 41 (November 1986), 809, 813, 815.

37. *The Record*, 42 (November 1987), 901.

38. Ibid., 907.

39. Summarized in "AIDS and the Criminal Justice System: Executive Summary of the Final Report," *The Record*, 44 (October 1989), 601.

40. Joint Subcommittee on AIDS in the Criminal Justice System, *AIDS and the Criminal Justice System: Final Report and Recommendations* (July 1989).

7

"Our Soul Is in *Pro Bono* Work": The City Bar, 1988–92

DURING THE PRESIDENCIES OF Sheldon Oliensis and Conrad Harper, the City Bar, through the Robert McKay Community Outreach Law Program, became more directly involved in providing legal services to the poor than ever before. Committed to a policy of inclusion and diversity with respect to the composition of its own staff and committees, the Association successfully pressed upon the large law firms and corporate law departments a statement committing the firms and departments to hiring minority lawyers in numbers equal to ten percent of all lawyers hired over the following five years and a further pledge to improve their rates of retention and promotion of minority lawyers. During these years the Association became much more involved with its own profession than it had been before, assisting lawyers who lost their jobs as a result of the economic recession that began toward the end of the 1980s, establishing guidelines for law firms for the termination of attorneys, and initiating a program to directly mediate or arbitrate disputes between attorneys. In addition, there were significant activities in two areas of traditional concern to the Association—criminal justice and municipal affairs.

THE PRESIDENCIES OF SHELDON OLIENSIS AND CONRAD HARPER

Sheldon "Jim" Oliensis was born in Philadelphia on March 19, 1922. He attended the University of Pennsylvania and the Harvard Law School, where he was president of the *Harvard Law Review*. After a period of practice with another firm, Oliensis joined Kaye Scholer Fierman Hays & Handler as a litigation partner in 1960. Oliensis chaired a number of Association committees, including State Legislation, Revision of the Constitution and Bylaws, Grievance (1975–78), and Access to Legal Services (1982–87). The Committee on Electric Power and the Environment, which he chaired from 1971 to 1974, produced a three-hundred-page working paper, "Electricity and the Environment: The Reform of Legal Institutions" in 1972. Oliensis also served as a member of the Grievance Committee, the Committee on the Judiciary, and the Ad Hoc Committee on Lawyer Advertising (1977–78). He was a member of the Executive Committee from 1961 to 1965 and vice president twice (1974–75, 1986–87). At the time of his election as president, he was chairing the Joint Committee on Fee Disputes and Conciliation of the City Bar, the New York County Lawyers' Association, and the Bronx County Bar.

Oliensis was deeply concerned with the provision of legal services to the poor. He chaired the Association's Committee on Legal Services, was a founder and president of VOLS (1984–87) and a director of New York Lawyers for the Public Interest, and had been vice president and president of Legal Aid. Oliensis has also been involved in other professional and civic affairs. He has been a trustee of the Lawyers' Committee for Civil Rights Under Law and a director of the Fund for Modern Courts. He has also been president of the New York City Park Association, director of the East Harlem Tutorial Program, a member of the Harvard Overseers Committee to visit the Law School and president of the Harvard Law School Association. After his service as president of the City Bar, Oliensis served as chair of the New York City Conflicts of Interest Board, succeeding former Association president Merrell Clark, Jr.[1]

The most important accomplishments of the Oliensis presidency were the increase in the number of committees from 120 to 150, covering virtually every subject area, and in the number of slots on committees, thereby increasing the opportunity for many more members to serve on committees; the institutionalization of diversity in the appointment of members to committees; the vast expansion of community outreach programs; and the launching of the Committee to Enhance Professional Opportunities for Minorities.[2]

Conrad K. Harper succeeded Oliensis as president in 1990. Harper, born in Detroit on December 2, 1940, is the son of an attorney and a former English teacher. A graduate of Howard University and of the Harvard Law School, Harper began his professional career with the NAACP Legal Defense Fund (1965–70). There, he worked on the Denver school desegregation case among others, the first school desegregation case decided by the Supreme Court in which segregation had not formally been ordered by law. Harper joined Simpson Thacher & Bartlett in 1971. When he became a partner in 1974, he and Amalya Kearse of Hughes Hubbard were the only African-American partners of a major New York corporate firm. At Simpson Thacher, Harper concentrated on litigation involving products liability, civil rights, securities, and environmental law. Harper was the fourth member of the firm of Simpson Thacher to head the Association (after Thomas Thacher, Whitney North Seymour, Sr., and Cyrus Vance).

Sponsored for membership by Francis Rivers, the first African-American member of the Association (1929) and the first African-American officer, Harper served on the Committees on Civil Rights, Federal Legislation (where he was the only one to dissent from that committee's initial refusal to endorse the Equal Rights Amendment), Judiciary, Children's Rights, Legal Education and Admission to the Bar, the Library Committee, and the Special Committee on the Second Century. From 1976 to 1980, he served on the Executive Committee, chairing it the last year he served (the first African-American to do so). Outside the Association, Harper was co-chair of the Lawyers' Committee for Civil Rights Under Law and chair of the Second Circuit Committee on Admissions and Grievances. He is a member of the American Law Institute and serves on ALI's Council. In 1977, as Special Consultant to the Department of Health Education & Welfare, Harper was instrumental in settling, after six months of negotiations, a twelve-year dispute over desegregation and bilingual education in the Chicago schools. A great bibliophile, Harper owns more than 5,000 books and has recently published an article on Jane Austen. He has been a trustee of the New York Public Library, the Museum of the City of New York, and Chancellor of the Episcopal Diocese of New York. Now Legal Advisor of the Department of State, Harper has been mentioned as a possible nominee for a seat on the U.S. Supreme Court.[3]

An inspirational president, Harper had his greatest achievements in improving racial and ethnic diversity in the profession and on the bench, expanding the Association's outreach activities, and successfully resisting the Department of Justice's efforts to exclude the Association from the evaluation of federal judicial nominees. He also secured funding for a substantial start on microfilming the Association's treasured collection of records and briefs of cases argued in the U.S. Courts of Appeals.

It is the Association's custom to accept portraits of its presidents for hanging on its walls. At the unveiling of his portrait, Harper delighted the assembled guests by saying, "It is a pleasure to add a little color to these walls."

THE ROBERT B. MCKAY COMMUNITY OUTREACH LAW PROGRAM

The Community Outreach Law Program (COLP), created in 1987 and named for Robert McKay after his death, has become a model for the creation and maintenance by a bar association of legal clinics providing direct service to diverse communities in an urban area. The roots of the City Bar's direct participation in providing legal services for the poor lie in the small ad hoc programs of the 1970s and 1980s. A Committee of Senior Volunteer Lawyers was formed in 1978 not only to assist senior citizens and prisoners, but also to serve the courts as arbitrators and masters and with lawyer discipline and to speak about the legal system in the schools.[4] In the early 1980s, the Committee on Immigration and Nationality Law co-sponsored all-day sessions for volunteer lawyers to assist them in the preparation and litigation of Haitian asylum-claims.[5] After passage of the 1986 Immigration Law, which provided a one-year amnesty for illegal immigrants during which they could achieve the status of legal residents, the Immigration and Nationality Law Committee not only organized counseling sessions for churches and neighborhood associations, but also trained lawyers and paralegal volunteers, who could assist aliens in completing their applications.[6] In a few months, six hundred people had attended counseling and training sessions.[7] The Association has continued to sponsor projects to assist refugees when they file applications for asylum and to represent them at hearings. There has been a more recent project for Haitian refugees seeking political asylum, another for Salvadorans and Guatemalans, and a third for those Chinese refugees seeking political asylum who had been passengers on the *Golden Venture*, which ran aground off Queens in 1993.

In his 1984–85 annual report, Robert McKay pointed to the Legal Assistance Committee, which had developed a program to provide assistance of counsel to tenants in Housing Court. Early in 1986, a pilot *pro bono* project for the New York City Housing Court, sponsored by the Committee on Legal Assistance, matching five law firms (including Simpson Thatcher and Shearman & Sterling) with Legal Services offices, had begun. The underlying purpose of the project was to determine whether the private bar could render effective and efficient service in Housing Court.[8] The attorneys were successful in obtaining court-ordered repairs and rent abatements, restoring people to their homes, obtaining leases, and winning dismissals of eviction proceedings. However, only 158 tenants were assisted by fifty-eight attorneys, a tiny fraction of those who needed assistance.[9]

In 1987 the Community Outreach Law Program (COLP) was created to provide legal information, referral services, and direct representation to the city's needy population. Each president since then has shared the view that it is important for the Association to expand beyond committees and staff to serve as lawyers to the poor.[10] Laurie Milder was the first staff member of COLP and director until 1994 and set up every program mentioned. She now serves as Special Counsel and continues her work in setting up the programs.

The pattern for development of outreach programs has been to focus upon a class of clients deprived of adequate legal services, then to structure a program to train volunteer lawyers. Those lawyers are matched with clients seeking assistance to provide either counseling or direct representation.[11] The Community Outreach Law Program often works with community groups and other legal services organizations to multiply its effect. Whenever possible, COLP offers basic legal training to service professionals. All the COLP programs are dependent upon a corps of volunteers recruited from the ranks of attorneys, law students, recent graduates, and paralegals.[12] The volunteer lawyers are trained and given mentor assistance, advice, paralegal support, and a library of resource materials.[13]

A few examples of COLP programs suggest their diversity and significance. The Hostos Center for Women's and Immigrants' Rights, which was awarded New York State Bar Association Award of Merit, is located in the South Bronx. Volunteer lawyers knowledgeable in family, housing, and immigration law train peer counselors and advocates, conduct counseling sessions with local residents, and participate in forums.[14]

In 1990 the Association sponsored two programs for summer associates: one in Housing Court, where volunteer law students would be enlisted to help tenants prepare and file the necessary papers to prevent eviction; the other aided battered wives in Family Court.[15] By 1993 more than 100 summer associates were participating in COLP programs.

The Association began its Monday Night Legal Advisory Workshops in 1991. Every Monday night, up to eight volunteer lawyers supervised by the Young Lawyers Committee provide assistance in many areas of the law to clients initially screened by the Association's Legal Referral Service. Between March 1991 and May 1993, one thousand persons were counseled by seventy-five different lawyers.[16]

There was a vast expansion of *pro bono* direct service activities in 1991–92, the second year of Harper's presidency and the year Thomas Moreland chaired the Executive Committee. That year 647 volunteer lawyers were trained, joining the 354 of the year before. Every one of the 1,001 trained volunteer lawyers had agreed to handle one *pro bono* matter.[17]

In 1992 the Guardian Ad Litem Program was launched, recruiting, training, and matching volunteer lawyers and nonlawyers with persons who are mentally impaired or otherwise incapable of defending their rights in Housing Court without a great risk of eviction. The guardians represent the tenant with his/her landlord and try to avoid eviction. By 1994, the Guardian Ad Litem Project covered all five boroughs.

One of the early medical-related COLP projects took place at Bellevue Hospital. There, hospital social workers were trained to identify legal issues of concern to patients and to provide them with basic information. If further advice proved necessary, social workers called a telephone helpline and would speak with an attorney with expertise in family, immigration, or elder law.

A number of new programs were created by McKay COLP during the 1992–93 year. In the areas of immigration law, elder law, family law, public benefits, and law-related education, 3,189 low-income persons were provided assistance. The largest of these programs, counseling for the homeless, is discussed in the next chapter. In the area of elder law, McKay COLP worked with the Association's Committee on Legal Problems of the Aging and the New York City Department for the Aging to develop a comprehensive training program encompassing financial and health care planning, security, government benefits, and consumer and housing problems. Six senior centers throughout the city are visited by two volunteers at least once a month.[18]

There was also a matrimonial law program in which each year the volunteers completing training were required to handle one contested divorce matter assigned by the Supreme Court. By the end of Conrad Harper's presidency, McKay COLP also encompassed bankruptcy, AIDS counseling, and domestic violence. In his Farewell Address, Harper said, "If our heart as an association is in the profession, our soul is in *pro bono* work."[19] When John Feerick gave his Farewell Address two years later, he referred to new COLP programs involving breast cancer patients (primarily dealing with disputes with insurance companies, guardianship for children, and preparation of health care proxies) and a project dealing with child custody and visitation matters.[20]

Late in Feerick's tenure, a Council on Public Service was established to coordinate the work of a number of existing and new committees, whose focus was to carry on a broad range of legal and nonlegal service projects. The purpose of the Public Service Council, as explained by Feerick, was "to infuse every part of the Association with the ethic of public service; to generate new activities all the time and to widely publicize what was being done to encourage others to follow that example."[21]

Among the COLP projects initiated since 1994 is the Cancer Advocacy Project (co-sponsored by the Association, McKay COLP, and the New York County Lawyers' Association) and a collaboration with

Women in Need (WIN) to provide legal assistance to homeless women and children.[22]

From 1987 to 1992, more than a thousand Association members volunteered in the COLP programs. In 1991, volunteers donated 12,600 hours to COLP projects. In the 1992 calendar year, McKay COLP staff trained 843 volunteer lawyers and served 1,835 clients directly. In 1992–93, 1,000 tenants were helped; 1,589 were served in the legal clinics; and many others had cases assigned to lawyers.[23]

The outreach program has produced publications aimed at recruiting attorneys, such as *Pro Bono Opportunities: A Guide for Lawyers in New York City* (1991) (earlier editions go back at least to 1980),[24] or helping those needing assistance, such as the *Tenant's Guide to the Housing Court* (1990), which has been distributed to thousands of people in each borough.

The 1989 State Bar Association Award of Merit was given to the Hostos Center for Women's and Immigrants' Rights program. In 1991 the McKay COLP won its second award from the ABA for its immigrant students' rights program, in which students, parents, and school staffs were advised about the legal rights of immigrants and a legal helpline is manned to answer questions from students, teachers, and guidance counselors. In 1993 the Immigrants' Legal Rights Project won the ABA Public Service Award.[25]

The Association's activities go beyond legal representation and advice and publications, and there are related programs with which COLP has not been involved. There is, for example, the Thurgood Marshall Summer Law Internship Program established in 1993 to give inner city high school students the opportunity to experience working in a legal environment through a paid summer job. That year, fifty law firms, sixteen law departments, and four law schools provided jobs for sixty-four students. There is the senior lawyers' Mentor Program, which matches students from New York high schools with lawyers who act as mentors and role models. One hundred attorneys are mentoring students from the Martin Luther King, Jr. High School,[26] meeting periodically one-on-one with the students (during the student's lunch hour) to talk about law or anything else on the individual student's mind. There is also the Lloyd K. Garrison Student Leadership Program, which awards fifteen internships to alternative high school students. There is also a law-related education project designed to introduce the students to various career options and to make them more aware of legal issues. Volunteer attorneys conduct classroom presentations on different areas of the law and organize field trips to courts and correctional facilities.[27] The Association also awards annual Legal Services Awards recognizing lawyers who provide outstanding legal assistance to the poor.

Assisting Minorities in the Profession

At the end of Conrad Harper's term as president, the Executive Committee adopted a policy of non-discrimination for the Association:

> The Association of the Bar of the City of New York is committed to a policy of inclusion and diversity with respect to the composition of its staff, its membership, the chairs and members of its committees, and its officers. Consistent with the policy of promoting inclusiveness and diversity, the Association does not discriminate against any individual because of such individual's actual or perceived race, color, creed, religion, national origin, gender, age, marital status, sexual orientation, disability, or alienage or citizenship status.[28]

During the years Sheldon Oliensis and Conrad Harper were presidents of the Association, the City Bar sought affirmatively to increase the impact of minorities within the Association and to increase the number of minority lawyers in the big firms and corporate departments.

Oliensis worked effectively to increase minority representation on Association committees. Following a suggestion of the Committee on Minorities in the Profession chaired by Merrell Clark, Jr., Oliensis urged all committee heads to assume responsibility for recruiting minorities for their committees. In Clark's view, the effort was a searching process to find well-qualified minorities which would then ensure minority representation on committees. This in turn would help recruit more minority members to the Association.[29]

Believing that all Association committees should have minority representation, except for the very few where it did not appear to be practical, Oliensis was willing to battle committee by committee. He was able to announce in his Farewell Address that the Association had minorities "on all but about a dozen of the standing and special committees of the Association and those few exceptions are in relatively esoteric fields," in which it was "still working hard to achieve minority representation on those committees as well."[30]

Oliensis also made substantial efforts to involve more women in the Association (discussed in the following chapter) and more young lawyers and to make the Association more user friendly for the disabled, including the purchase of a machine for the library which can read to blind lawyers.

Even more important were the efforts made to increase the number of minorities in the large law firms and corporate departments. In 1974 Conrad Harper was one of only two African-American partners of Wall Street firms. A decade later, the number had risen to only seven. Even in 1991, of the sixty-two firms in New York City with seventy-five attorneys or more—firms with a total of 3,642 partners—there were only twenty African-American and nine Asian-American partners.[31]

The Committee on Minorities in the Profession was established in 1984, with Joseph Barbash as its first chair. The committee established a liaison with minority bar associations, attended their meetings, and invited their members to attend meetings at the Association and to become Association members.[32] Shortly after Oliensis became president, the committee reported the results of its intensive review of the recruitment and hiring process and recommended ways the process could be improved.

Oliensis met with the partners of every major Wall Street firm and later appointed a committee charged with identifying, developing, and implementing means of increasing the opportunities for minorities to enter and advance in the legal profession.[33] Cyrus Vance was named to chair the Committee to Enhance Professional Opportunities for Minorities, which had as its members the heads of thirty-five major firms.

Under Vance, with the important assistance of Arthur Liman who chaired the drafting subcommittee, the committee drew up a "Statement of Goals on Minority Hiring and Promotion."[34] The signatories—initially 131 law firms and 41 corporations—pledged themselves to hire a substantial number of minority lawyers (African-American, Asian-American, Hispanic-American, and Native American) and declared as a desirable goal the hiring of minority lawyers equal to ten percent of all lawyers hired over the next five years. They further pledged to improve their rates of retaining and promoting minority lawyers. In the preface, Conrad Harper eloquently took note of the fact that "leaders of the Bar have not been content merely to have the Association speak in its own name"; "instead, by an act of unmistakable clarity and institutional seriousness, law firms have affirmed their adherence to the Statement of Goals unanimously adopted by the 35-member Committee. . . ."[35] A Special Committee on Government Counsel, chaired by Jeffrey Friedlander, issued its own statement on goals for governmental and quasi-governmental legal departments.[36]

About a half-year later, a subcommittee on retention of the Vance Committee, chaired by Ira M. Millstein, issued a report containing the results of a survey of minority lawyers at nineteen of the thirty-five firms making up the Vance Committee. The report documented the perception of African-American lawyers that their situation was different from that of their colleagues. Sixty-one percent of African-American lawyers reported that their work experience was different from their non-minority colleagues. Seventy-four percent reported disparities between their relationships with minority and non-minority colleagues. The report called for fast action to effect specific remedies, including diversity training, improved evaluation procedures, and the employment at the Association of an Assistant to the President for Improving Promotion and Retention of Minorities in the Profession, who would work closely with the committee to enhance professional opportunities and help firms and corporate law departments to secure the hiring, retention, and promotion of minority lawyers. Suzanne Baer was named to the position, which was funded by grants of $5,000 from each of the law firms represented on the Vance Committee.[37]

Conrad Harper made a major effort to make the Association multiracial.* On his watch, the Vance Committee's Statement of Goals and the reports of both the Millstein Subcommittee and the Special Committee on Government Counsel were rendered, as was the Executive Committee's statement on inclusion and diversity within the Association. In addition, in February 1991 Harper spoke out vigorously about the "virtual disappearance of minority judges from the federal trial benches" of the city. At the time, there was a total of one African-American judge in full-time service and two on senior status in the Southern and Eastern Districts together. No African-American lawyer had been appointed to either bench between 1978 and 1991, although two Hispanic-Americans had been appointed in the Southern District.[38] In December 1991, an all-day conference sponsored by the Committee to Encourage Judicial Service brought hundreds of minority lawyers to the Association for discussions of how to be a judge. A program for minority law students in New York area law schools was begun in 1991 with one first-year student from each law school placed with a large law firm as a paid summer associate. The selection of each student was done by the Association from a list of four to six students provided by each law school. Three fellowships in environmental law for minority students were awarded for summer work and a Thurgood Marshall Fellowship for law students committed to public service was established.[39]

THE ASSOCIATION AND THE PROFESSION, 1988–92

There were vast changes in the practice of law during the 1980s. Toward the end of the decade, the Association became increasingly involved with its profession, especially in assisting lawyers who had lost their jobs as the result of the economic recession.

During the 1980s, new attorneys continued to pour out of law schools. Large law firms grew and grew. Between 1975 and 1987, the

---

*Years before he was president of the Association, Harper's offer to buy a home in Irvington, New York, had been accepted. Then, suddenly, the home was taken off the market. With the backing of his law partners, Harper won an injunction to prevent the house from being sold to someone else. He ultimately settled the lawsuit which followed and bought the house.

number of firms in the United States with at least 100 lawyers increased from 47 to 245 and the number of attorneys in those firms increased from 6,558 to 51,851.[40] But, the market was unstable. There was intense competition for clients and a drifting away from permanent lawyer-client relationships. At the same time, corporate in-house legal departments were growing rapidly, and clients were becoming more fee-conscious. Departments of law firms broke off to become boutiques. Some old firms, like Greenbaum Wolf & Ernst, died, while even some of the skyrocketing new firms, like Finley Kumble, collapsed. The increased competitiveness began to sharply affect the quality of life of attorneys. The most successful firms relied more and more heavily on associates, who were forced to work sweatshop hours and wait longer to become partners (and a larger percentage did *not* become partners). In 1992, John Feerick described the challenge facing the profession:

> Lawyers increasingly question whether legal careers are worth the price and lament not having sufficient time for family or service to the community. Minority and women lawyers express frustration at the continued difficulties they encounter which prevent them from advancing to the highest levels of our profession and erode their self-confidence. Lawyers of my generation too frequently speak of a decline in civility and ethics. . . . And, law students have become apprehensive about the viability of long-term careers in the law.[41]

Finally, a severe recession in the profession of law in the New York area struck in the late 1980s. Between 1990 and November 1992, there was a decline of 8,000 positions in the New York legal community (including support personnel).

The Committee on Lawyers in Transition was created in 1990. Madeline Stoller became its first chair. The Association's Lawyers in Transition Program is believed to be one of the largest and most active in the country as the committee is reinforced with two staff positions. Naomi Tate became the first project coordinator. The program has offered workshops on résumé-writing techniques and networking; a mentoring project in which experienced lawyers are matched with lawyers in transition to help the latter stay plugged into the legal community; inexpensive listings in *44th Street Notes*; reference materials, a manual and job bulletin board; group therapy sessions as well as a referral list of psychologists who have worked with lawyers in the past. In addition, while unemployed, lawyers may still gain experience by handling matters on a *pro bono* basis for The Legal Aid Society, the New York City Law Department, and Legal Services for the Elderly.[42]

The Association has also adopted "Guidelines Regarding Terminations of Attorneys at Law Firms." Perhaps the most important such guideline was promulgated to prevent law firms from claiming that firings were the result of the disappointing performance of the fired attorney when actually they were reductions for economic reasons:

> . . . a law firm should not state or imply that a termination caused essentially by economic considerations was based on performance evaluations. . . . When an attorney's termination results from the application of new performance standards, or an acceleration of review procedures adopted because of a decline in the firm's business, the decision to terminate an attorney at that time is plainly attributable to the firm's economic circumstances. To represent the decision as having been based on the attorney's professional performance is unfair.[43]

The "Guidelines" were sent to 150 New York law firms. In addition, on April 20, 1991, there was a conference at the House on "How to Survive the Shake-Out in the Lawyers' Marketplace."

A very different professional problem was raised by the lawsuit brought by the Office of Thrift Supervision against Kaye, Scholer, Fierman, Hays & Handler, freezing most of the firm's assets. OTS brought suit on March 2, 1992, against the law firm and three partners for $275 million, claiming the firm misled regulators while representing Charles Keating's Lincoln Savings and Loan Association. No hearing took place before the freeze went into effect. On March 8, the firm settled with the agency for $41 million (about half of that was covered by insurance). The firm claimed that the information that OTS said Kaye Scholer had wrongfully withheld would have violated state ethics rules had it been disclosed. Within weeks of the episode, a forum was held at the House. That was followed by a report of the Committee on Professional Responsibility which stated that asset freezes in law firms "impair the firm's ability to represent its clients, threaten the attorney-client privilege and create unique hardships which all but force capitulation." The committee recommended that OTS be required to secure the approval of a federal judge before freezing a law firm's assets, and that the government be required to show both a substantial likelihood of success at trial on the merits *and* extraordinary circumstances which indicate that the defendant is disposing of assets to such an extent as to make an ultimate judgment uncollectible. Nevertheless, the report was less supportive of Kaye Scholer than some members of the Association would have liked.[44]

Another professional concern was civility. The Subcommittee on Advocacy Misconduct of the Criminal Advocacy Committee conducted a survey of all the state and federal judges in New York City hearing criminal cases. The results of the survey were disturbing. Of the 123 judges who responded, 47 percent considered attorney misconduct (improper summations, lateness, the baiting and insulting of witnesses, and intentional violation or evasion of the rules of the court) to be a serious problem in their courtroom. Two-thirds of the judges indicated that existing sanctions against misconduct were of little use in dealing with defense attorneys and half said the same regarding prosecutors.[45]

In June 1988 the Federal Courts Committee dealt with another piece of the civility problem—"hardball" litigation tactics. Beginning with the premise that "the level of civility among lawyers is not what it should be," the committee recommended a code of litigation conduct in areas subject to abuse, including such matters as adjustments and extensions of time, the timing and manner of the service of papers, written submissions relying on materials not in the record, depositions, document demands, and settlement practices.[46]

Still another area in which the Association has been working is mediation and arbitration of disputes between lawyers. The program, created initially to deal with the breakup and demise of large law partnerships accompanied by proliferation of litigation among lawyers, has expanded to deal with other intra-professional disputes.[47]

Among the other professional matters considered by committees in recent years have been the proposed amendments to Rule 11 of Federal Rules of Civil Procedure (which provide sanctions for papers filed in federal court under some circumstances) and the funding of the state's disciplinary and grievance committees. In addition, the 1993 Leslie Arps Memorial Lecture addressed the subject "Law Practice: A Profession or Regulated Industry?" The speaker was the 89-year-old Herbert Brownell.[48]

In recent years the Association has invested an increasing amount of attention to the challenge confronting "our City of New York." In 1992, President John Feerick called for "all committees, councils and delegations to commit an increasing level of their energy and imagination to New York City."[49] Many of the outreach efforts, if not all, aim, of course, at helping different communities within the city. But the city was also attracting Association attention in other ways.

Even before Feerick's presidency, increased activity in municipal matters was noticeable. In the late 1980s the Association was an active participant in the thinking and debate over revision of the New York Charter. When New York State's intricate rules for ballot access through petition once again caused turmoil and hardship—the legitimacy of many of the candidacies had not been determined until shortly before the mayoral primary in 1985—the successful candidate, Edward I. Koch, asked the Association to study the state's election law with its highly technical restrictions on access to the ballot. The Special Committee on Election Law was established in response in September 1985. Marilyn F. Friedman chaired the committee, which included as members Robert M. Kaufman, Victor Kovner, Standish Forde Medina, Jr., Monroe E. Price, and Michael D. Stallman. The committee's final report, "Ballot Access in New York," rendered in 1989, was a comprehensive analysis of the petition process, the objection process, and the litigation process. (Two of the reports had been released in earlier years.)

In "The Petition Process," the committee reviewed the complex maze of rules dealing with petition signature requirements for designation in primary and general elections. In "The Objection Process," the committee examined the procedures of the Board of Elections. In "The Litigation Process," the committee examined the judicial treatment of petition cases, concluding that the process "often strains the professionalism, competence and dignity of all who participate in it." The committee set forth a blueprint to reform the access process and made a comprehensive series of recommendations to eliminate pitfalls from the statutory petition rules; critically analyzed the Board of Elections' procedures with regard to objections to petitions, recommending substantial simplification of the process; and made recommendations about the litigation process—the problems of which the Committee concluded stem in large measure from the petition process itself.[50]

Just before Sheldon Oliensis became president, the Committee on Municipal Affairs reported on the New York City Department of Investigation, which had been embarrassed by revelations of corruption within the Parking Violations Bureau, a scandal that came to light in January 1986 when the Borough President of Queens committed suicide. The committee called for enhancing the Department of Investigation's independence, extension of its jurisdiction, broadening of the local whistle-blowing statute, and greater concern by the D.O.I. for due process rights.[51]

The city's schools were of continued interest. In June 1988, after the failure of efforts to return the Board of Education to mayoral control, the Committee on Education and the Law, clearly aware that "an appropriate system of governance" would not in itself "necessarily improve the education" of public school students, and that "the City Board appears to be part of the problem," presented a working paper on alternatives to the existing board.[52] Less than a week after Joseph A. Fernandez became schools chancellor, a study by the Committee on Municipal Affairs reported on a disciplinary system so ineffective that incompetent principals were not removed from their schools. In ten years, only eight principals had been brought up on charges. The committee recommended changing the state law to give the chancellor ultimate authority to dismiss them.[53] On a narrower, but still important and controversial, subject, President Harper, writing at the recommendation of the Committees on Sex and Law, Medicine and Law, and Education and the Law, voiced Association support of Chancellor Fernandez's proposal to make condoms available in high schools.[54]

In 1990, the *Record* published as a report what originally had been a letter to the new mayor, David Dinkins, from the Committee on Corrections. Reporting on the conditions of the court pens operated by the Department of Correction, the committee described how those held two or three days in the pens (and still presumed innocent) lacked facilities to wash, shower, shave, and brush their teeth. They wrote of toilets stuffed with excrement and of so much overcrowding that there was competition for space on the concrete floors just to lie down and rest. The Committee urged the mayor to appoint someone with power to coordinate and control the entire prearraignment process.[55]

The Committee on Transportation, considering freight a crucial component of economic competitiveness, addressed in 1990 the problem of freight movement in the New York region. The committee concluded that the New York region's system of freight movement was in crisis, that its present inability to move goods appropriately and efficiently had bled the region of industry and jobs, and depleted its wealth, and was threatening to "write its economic epitaph." The committee recommended a series of actions including the establishment of a regional freight authority charged with diverting freight from overburdened highways, the consolidation of east-of-Hudson rail operations, and the completion and enhancement of the New York State Full Freight Access Program.[56]

In a 1992 report the Committee on the Civil Court highlighted the devastating effects of budgetary cuts on that court. A court of limited jurisdiction hearing relatively simple claims not exceeding $25,000—commercial, landlord/tenant, and tort cases—the Civil Court is relied upon by banks, landlords, and companies seeking to effect collection of consumer and other debts. In 1991, 230,402 cases were filed in the Civil Court, 55,186 of which were small-claims cases. That year budget cuts of nine percent caused an eighteen percent reduction of non-judicial staff; this, in turn, led to suspension of the compulsory arbitration program, enormous delays in the entering of judgments, and radical curtailment of the Small Claims Part. The committee indicated that the cuts had changed the function of the Civil Court as the "People's Court" and potentially would damage the municipal economy. After the report was written, a new budget was put into effect and matters improved somewhat.[57]

COMMITTEES

During the period when Sheldon Oliensis and Conrad Harper were president of the Association, the number of committees increased to more than 150, with most of the increase occurring during Oliensis's tenure. Oliensis sought to have committees function in every area the Association could function, in order to be able to increase the number of available slots for committee membership. During this time the number of slots increased by more than eight hundred. Take, for example, an area like tax law, which was served by but one committee when Oliensis became president. By the end of his presidency there were six committees handling different areas of tax law, as well as a Council on Taxation. Among the other committees created were the Special Committee on Government Ethics, chaired by M. Bernard Aidinoff, intended to address a broad spectrum of matters including campaign financing and conduct, financial disclosure, conflicts of interest, and the enforcement of ethics laws. There was a new Special Committee on Asian Affairs as well as committees on Sports Law and Construction Law. During his tenure Oliensis also attempted to increase the level of liaison activity of the Executive Committee, each member of which was assigned six to ten committees. Oliensis sought to make the Executive Committee a resource for the committees and a channel between the president and the committees.[58]

During Harper's presidency, there would be such new committees as those on Bioethics, Eastern European Affairs, and African Affairs as well as a Special Committee on Government Counsel. Under Harper, there was also a concerted effort to ensure that each committee had at least five members who were not specialists in the committee's subject matter, five lawyers admitted to the bar less than five to eight years, five female members, and two minority members.[59]

During the Oliensis–Harper period, the Committee on Federal Legislation reported on federal term limits, taking the position that they may be imposed only by constitutional amendment and that, as a matter of policy, term limits were not the most effective way to achieve federal campaign reform.[60]

The Association has had a long history of opposition to capital punishment. Although prior to 1995 there had not been any capital cases in New York for a generation, many members of the Association represented *pro bono* prisoners faced with execution in other states. The Association has conducted a series of continuing legal education programs for these lawyers. In 1989 the Committee on Civil Rights once again disapproved proposed New York State death penalty legislation, "because the committee continues to believe that capital punishment has no place in the American criminal justice system." The committee, chaired by Jonathan Lang, stated that capital punishment is "expensive, inefficient, unfair to minorities and the poor, and not a demonstrated deterrent to future murderers."[61] Later the same year the Committee on Civil Rights reviewed bills that emanated from the work of a U.S. Judicial Conference committee (chaired by former Justice Lewis F. Powell, Jr.) and were intended to create special procedures for federal habeas corpus litigation in capital cases. The Association committee took the position that "for so long as the death penalty continues to exist in this country, capital inmates are entitled to procedures . . . that result in the full and fair review of their convictions and sentences."[62]

Among the other reports of particular interest during these years was that of the Committee on Savings Institutions which sharply criticized a proposed FDIC regulation of "golden parachute payments";[63] that of the Committee on Legal Problems of the Aging which demonstrated that there were extensive problems with the structure of the statutes and processes intended to effectuate conservatorship;[64] that of the Civil Rights Committee which strongly criticized the restraints imposed upon journalists attempting to cover the Gulf War;[65] as well as the massive report of the Ad Hoc Committee on Medical Malpractice (summarized in *The Record*)[66] and that of the Committee on Administrative Law on Administrative Closings and Churning of Welfare Cases.[67]

THE LIBRARY

By the end of Conrad Harper's presidency the holdings of the Association's library, the jewel in its crown, numbered more than 600,000 volumes. Harper, perhaps the greatest bibliophile in the Association's history, spurred a campaign to fund the microfilming of the library's collection of records and briefs of the U.S. Courts of Appeals, which is rivaled only by those of the National Archives and the Library of Congress. Microfilming will not only preserve the collection, but make it available for sale to other law libraries.[68] The filming has begun with more than ten million pages of records and briefs of the Second Circuit.

On April 17, 1990, Anthony P. Grech, Librarian and Curator, who had been on the Association's staff since 1949, died of a heart attack at the age of fifty-nine while walking to work. Beginning as a weekend page, Grech earned his undergraduate degree from Manhattan College and became a reference assistant in the library. He then earned his Masters in Library Science degree from Columbia University. From 1965 to 1967, Grech was the reference librarian. He was Librarian from 1967 to 1984 and, from 1984 until his death, was Librarian and Curator. His bibliographies on various subjects, like those of his predecessor, Joseph L. Andrews, were a constant feature of *The Record*, winning him the Joseph L. Andrews Bibliography Award in 1967. He had been president of the Law Library Association of Greater New York and a member of the Executive Board of the American Association of Law Libraries. The Distinguished Service Award was bestowed on him posthumously by the American Association of Law Librarians, and the Law Library Association of Greater New York named its annual scholarship for him.[69]

NOTES

1. *New York Times*, April 16, 1973; Robert Kaufman, "Letter from the President," *44th Street Notes*, 3, No. 5 (May 1988) 1, 2.

2. Sheldon Oliensis, "Farewell Address," *The Record*, 45 (May 1990), 414.

3. *44th Street Notes*, 4, No. 6 (June 1990), 1.

4. *The Record*, 35, No. 7 (October 1980), Supplement, p. 92.

5. Letter from Arthur C. Helton to Fern Schair received June 1984 (on file in the Association library).

6. Robert M. Kaufman, "Second Inaugural Address," *The Record*, 42 (June 1987), 593. See also Robert M. Kaufman, "Report of the President," *The Record*, 42 (October 1987), 744, 759.

7. *44th Street Notes*, 2, No. 9 (October 1987), 6.

8. See Robert McKay, "Report of the President," *The Record*, 40 (October 1985), 431; *The Record*, 42 (January/February 1987), 4–5.

9. Committee on Legal Assistance, "The Manhattan *Pro Bono* Housing Court Project," *The Record*, 44 (April 1989), 254ff.; interview with Thomas H. Moreland (see above, chap. 6, note 2).

10. *The Record*, 46 (May 1991), 349–50.

11. *The Record*, 50 (April 1995), 258.

12. Association of the Bar of the City of New York Fund, Inc., "Helping the Association Serve . . . ," (1993–94 Annual Report) p. 2.

13. *44th Street Notes*, 7, No. 8 (October 1992), 22.

14. Conrad K. Harper, "President's Column: *Pro Bono Publico*," *44th Street Notes*, 6, No. 1 (January 1991), 1, 2.

15. *New York Law Journal*, June 18, 1990.

16. John D. Feerick, "Second Inaugural Address, May 25, 1993," *The Record*, 48 (June 1993), 528.

17. Conrad K. Harper, "Second Inaugural Address," *The Record*, 46 (May 1991), 353, 354.

18. Laurie B. Milder, "In-House Perspectives: Caring for New Yorkers Through the Law," *Metropolitan Corporate Counsel*, 1, No. 2 (October 1993).

19. Conrad K. Harper, "Farewell Address, May 26, 1992," *The Record*, 47 (October 1992), 584, 587.

20. John D. Feerick, "Farewell Address," *The Record*, 49 (December 1994), 920, 922. See also *44th Street Notes*, 7, No. 10 (December 1992), 9.

21. *The Record*, 49 (March 1994), 130–31; interview with John D. Feerick (see above, chap. 1, note 2).

22. Association of the Bar of the City of New York Fund, Inc., "Helping the Asssociation Serve" (see above, note 12), p. 3; *The Record*, 49 (November 1994), 798.

23. *44th Street Notes*, 7, No. 10 (December 1992), 1; Association of the Bar of the City of New York Fund, Inc., 1992–93 Annual Report, pp. 2ff.; John D. Feerick, "Second Inaugural Address" (see above, note 16), 525, 529.

24. See *The Record*, 46 (October 1991), 486.

25. *44th Street Notes*, 7, No. 4 (April 1992) 8; *The Record*, 47 (March 1992), 114–15.

26. Interview with John D. Feerick, *Metropolitan Corporation Counsel*, 1, No. 2 (October 1993).

27. Laurie B. Milder, "In-House Perspective: Caring for New Yorkers through the Law" (see above, note 18).

28. *The Record*, 47 (May 1992), 352.

29. *Manhattan Lawyer*, January 10–January 16, 1989, p. 4. See also Sheldon Oliensis, "Farewell Address" (see above, note 2), 414, 416.

30. Ibid., 416.

31. Abel, *American Lawyers* (see above, chap. 3, note 33), pp. 106, 110–11; Hoffman, *Lions in the Street* (see above, chap. 4, note 4), p. 137; Conrad K. Harper, "Inaugural Address," *The Record*, 45 (May 1990), 425. Conrad K. Harper, "Second Inaugural Address" (see above, note 17) 353.

32. *44th Street Notes*, 3, No. 9 (November 1988), 1.

33. *The Record*, 45 (April 1990), 286.

34. Committee to Enhance Professional Opportunities for Minorities, "Statement of Goals of New York Law Firms and Corporate Legal Counsel Departments for Increasing Minority Hiring, Retention and Promotion," *The Record*, 46 (November 1991), 720.

35. Ibid.

36. Harper, "Farewell Address" (see above, note 19), 585.

37. Subcommittee on Retention of the Committee to Enhance Professional Opportunities for Minorities, "Report on the Retention of Minority Lawyers in the Profession," *The Record*, 47 (May 1992), 355.

38. *44th Street Notes*, 6, No. 2 (February 1991); Conrad K. Harper, "Integrate the Federal Bench," *New York Times*, February 22, 1991.

39. Harper, "Farewell Address" (see above, note 18), 585–86.

40. Abel, *American Lawyers* (see above, chap. 3, note 33), pp. 9, 10.

41. John D. Feerick, "President's Column: To a Rededication of our Efforts," *44th Street Notes*, 7, No. 7 (September 1992), 2.

42. John D. Feerick, "President's Column: Lawyers in Transition: An Association Program," *44th Street Notes*, 7, No. 9 (November 1992), 1–2.

43. Executive Committee, "Guidelines Regarding Terminations of Attorneys at Law Firms," *The Record*, 46 (October 1991), 595, 596.

44. Committee on Professional Responsibility, "Attachment of Law Firm Assets by Federal Regulatory Agencies," *The Record*, 47 (March 1992), 116; *New York Law Journal*, April 1, 1992. See also *New York Law Journal*, March 23, 1992.

45. *The Record*, 44 (October 1989), 572.

46. Committee on Federal Courts, "A Proposed Code of Litigation Conduct," *The Record*, 43 (October 1988), 738.

47. Committee on Arbitration and Alternative Dispute Resolution, "Proposal for Association-Sponsored Arbitration of Disputes Among Lawyers," *The Record*, 42 (November 1987), 877; "Association-Sponsored Mediation and Arbitration of Disputes Between Lawyers" (June 1991) (separate pamphlet).

48. *The Record*, 48 (December 1993), 965.

49. John D. Feerick, "Inaugural Address," *The Record*, 47 (October 1992), 589, 591.

50. [Association] press release, November 3, 1989. The reports are contained in *The Record*, 41 (October 1986), 710; *The Record*, 43 (January/February 1988), 7; *The Record*, 44 (November 1989), 731. The quotation is from the last report, p. 738.

51. Committee on Municipal Affairs, "Report on the New York City Department of Investigation," *The Record*, 43 (December 1988), 948; Association of the Bar of the City of New York News Release, May 19, 1988.

52. Committee on Education and the Law, "New York City Board of Education Governance Alternatives," *The Record*, 44 (January/February 1989), 25.

53. New York *Daily News*, September 29, 1989, p. 26; *Newsday*, September 29, 1989 and October 2, 1989, pp. 7, 21.

54. *The Record*, 46 (March 1991), 209–10.

55. Committee on Corrections, "Inadequacies in New York City Court Prearraignment Pens," *The Record*, 45 (April 1990), 390.

56. Committee on Transportation, "For Whom the Bell Tolls: New York's Mortal Crisis in Goods Movement," *The Record*, 46 (November 1991), 795; Sheldon Oliensis, "Letter from the President: Diversity of the Association's Committees," *44th Street Notes*, 5, No. 5 (May 1990), 2.

57. Committee on the Civil Court of the City of New York, "The State of the New York City Civil Court," *The Record*, 47 (March 1992), 176, 177, 181, note.

58. Sheldon Oliensis, "Farewell Address" (see above, note 2), 414.

59. Conrad K. Harper, "President's Column," *44th Street Notes*, 5, No. 8 (October 1990), 1, 2.

60. Committee on Federal Legislation, "Term Limits for United States Representatives and Senators," *The Record*, 46 (November 1991), 755.

61. Committee on Civil Rights, "Statement on Proposed New York Death-Penalty Legislation," *The Record*, 44 (June 1989), 516.

62. Committee on Civil Rights, "Legislative Modification of Federal Habeas Corpus in Capital Cases," *The Record*, 44 (December 1989), 848. See also Committee on Civil Rights, "The Death Penalty," *The Record*, 39 (October 1984), 419.

63. "Comments on the Proposed Regulation of Golden Parachute Payments and Other Benefits Subject to Misuse," *The Record*, 47 (April 1992), 315.

64. "Conservatorship in New York State: Does It Serve the Needs of the Elderly?" *The Record*, 45 (April 1990), 288.

65. "Military Restrictions on Press Coverage: The Unacceptability of the Pentagon's Policies During the Persian Gulf Conflict," *The Record*, 46 (December 1991), 843.

66. "Medical Malpractice Recommendations for the State of New York: Executive Summary," *The Record*, 45 (June 1990), 573.

67. *The Record*, 45 (April 1990), 379.

68. *44th Street Notes*, 6, No. 8 (October 1991), 1.

69. "President's Column," *44th Street Notes*, 5, No. 7 (September 1990), 1; F. S. Baum, "The Library," *44th Street Notes*, 6, No. 8 (October 1991), 3.

8

"To Infuse Every Part of the Association with the Ethic of Public Service": The City Bar in the 1990s

DURING THE PAST THREE YEARS, the City Bar has remained on the course fixed in the 1980s—increased legal services for the poor, assisting minorities within the profession, diversity within the Association—while the two presidents, John D. Feerick and Barbara Paul Robinson, added goals of their own. Feerick sought to enhance the quality of life in the city, galvanize public support for higher ethical standards for public officials, and involve more law professors and law students in the Association. Robinson, the fifty-seventh Association president and the first woman president, sought to use her office most particularly to assist young people and women in the profession of law. This chapter considers not only the significant activities from 1992 to date, but also developments in the area of gender discrimination within the Association over the past quarter-of-a-century, the efforts of the Association to prevent discrimination on the basis of sexual orientation over the same period, and more recent efforts to provide legal advice to the homeless.

THE PRESIDENTS: JOHN D. FEERICK AND BARBARA PAUL ROBINSON

Dean of Fordham Law School since 1982, John D. Feerick is the third "academic" to head the Association.* Feerick also had a sub-

---

*After Russell Niles and Robert McKay.

stantial career in practice—twenty-one years at Skadden Arps Slate Meagher & Flom, where he specialized in labor law and litigation. Feerick was born in New York City on July 12, 1936, the son of Irish immigrants, to whom he dedicated his presidency, for they had died just before he began it. Feerick is a graduate of Fordham College and Fordham Law School, where he was editor-in-chief of the law review. As a young scholar, Feerick studied the problem of disability in the office of President of the United States. He wrote law review articles and a book on the subject and ultimately became a major participant in the drafting of the Twenty-Fifth Amendment to the U.S. Constitution.[1] Feerick has also been a strong advocate of direct election of the President of the United States and a strong opponent of methods of disciplining federal judges by means other than impeachment. Active in a variety of municipal and state commissions, Feerick chaired the New York State Commission on Government Integrity (1987–90). For three and one-half years that panel looked into campaign financing, patronage, contracting practices, conflicts of interest involving state officials, and the protection of "whistle blowers," producing a 743-page volume of reports. One of Feerick's concerns as president of the Association was to use that podium to galvanize public opinion to force public officials to enact the reforms recommended by the Ethics Commission. Active in the Association, Feerick chaired the Committee on Federal Legislation and the Executive Committee and also served as vice president. Furthermore, he has been appointed Chairman of the Fund for Modern Courts.[2]

As president, Feerick worked hard to recruit law faculty to the Association. Twenty-two professors and academic administrators chaired committees during Feerick's presidency. Desiring to involve law students and recent graduates of law schools, Feerick successfully sought a change in the Association's bylaws to permit recent law school graduates to become members before their admission to the bar. Networking receptions were held for recent graduates, and a Law Student Perspectives Committee was set up with a quarterly newsletter. Another interest of Feerick's as president was the development of a technology center in the Association library. Deeply concerned with "the lawyers who had been let go," he formed the idea of creating the Lawyers in Transition Program (p. 145) and he stimulated similar activities by the New York State Bar Association. President during an economic recession, when bar associations throughout the country were losing members, Feerick worked successfully to develop systems to keep members from dropping out. The Association actually grew in membership during his incumbency.

Seeking to "give some energy to an already energetic association," Feerick saw the *pro bono* activities of the Association as a way to enhance the quality of life in New York City. He was responsible for the creation of the Council on Public Service to foster projects to aid residents of the city as well as to engage younger lawyers.[3] Serving as full-time dean of Fordham Law School while president, Feerick spent about 2,000 hours on Association business during his first year as president. Known for his sense of public duty and "goodness of spirit" (at Skadden, he was known as "Saint John"; at the Association, as "John the Good"), Feerick sought as president, in the words of Conrad Harper, to honor his "commitment to making sure that we are true to our founders."[4]

Barbara Paul Robinson grew up in Great Neck, Long Island. She graduated from Bryn Mawr and Yale Law School, where she was one of seven women in her class and an editor of the law journal. Joining Debevoise & Plimpton as an associate in 1966, Robinson pioneered the firm's "flextime" program in 1967 following the birth of her first child. She became the first woman partner at Debevoise (and the third Debevoise partner to serve as Association president during this period). Robinson's practice has focused primarily in the area of trusts and estates and providing counsel to tax-exempt organizations.[5]

At the City Bar, Robinson has served on the committees on judicial administration, as co-chair of the Joint Committee on Child Abuse, and as chair of the Committee on the Family Court and Family Law, the Nominating Committee, and the Committee on Trusts, Estates and Surrogates' Courts. She was a member of the Executive Committee from 1986 to 1990, its chair from 1989 to 1990, and vice president of the Association (1990–91).

In her inaugural address, Robinson made clear that a major concern of her presidency would be the disadvantaged young. "When we fail our young people," she said, "we can predict that they will fail us, that they will fail to become productive, law-abiding members of society." To invest in our young people while there is still a chance to reach them is essential, Robinson thought. A second, important concern of hers has been to assist women in the profession of law.[6]

In 1995, Robinson established a Council on Children, chaired by Michael Iovenko. At a budget-cutting time for governments, Robinson saw the council as beginning "the more difficult task of thinking about ways to analyze funding streams and to change delivery systems in order to provide better outcomes for children more effectively and efficiently."[7]

A second concern has been diversity. Robinson established two new task forces, one addressing minorities in the profession, the other dealing with women in the profession. "There is much employers can do," Robinson said in her Inaugural Address, "that will make a difference to younger women making their way, and, in particular, women who are trying to balance the demands of family with their professional commitments. . . . As I look at my own grown sons, of whom I am so proud, I firmly believe women should be able to choose to have both."[8]

The election of Barbara Robinson to the presidency of the City Bar reflected the large number of women entering the legal profession in the 1970s and 1980s, as well as the growth of women in leadership positions in the Association.

Until the 1970s, less than five percent of the profession were women. That changed rapidly in the late 1960s and 1970s. Between 1967 and 1983 the enrollment of women in ABA-approved law schools increased 1650 percent. While all law school applications were increasing threefold in the early 1970s, applications from women increased fourteenfold. By 1983, 37.7 percent of all law students were women. In 1995, women made up almost 43 percent of all law school graduates.

Although there was an extraordinary increase in the number of women lawyers in large firms during the 1970s, the number of women partners has trailed behind. There was only one woman partner in any large New York City firm in 1964; 34 in 1979; 41 in 1980. In the thirty-two largest firms in 1980, only 1.9 percent of partners were women.[9]

Changes in the Association came more rapidly than on Wall Street and so far have gone further. The first female member was not elected until 1937 (an event commemorated in 1987 with a dinner). In the 1950s and 1960s women were generally relegated to committees concerned with family law matters. Progress began to be made in the Plimpton–Botein years. The presence of women was particularly felt in two of the new committees—Consumer Affairs and Sex and Law. By the end of the decade, women were sitting on almost all the major substantive and procedural committees, although they occupied only 7.5 percent of all committee slots and chaired only nine committees (of which two—State Legislation and Corporation Law—were traditionally viewed as among the most important).[10]

Substantial progress was made during the 1980s. Fern Schair, no small figure in the life of the Association, was appointed Executive Secretary in 1982. Among the women chairs during the first year of Robert Kaufman's presidency—many of whom were appointed by Robert McKay—were Beatrice Shainswit (Tort Litigation), Madeline C. Stoller (Product Liability), Bettina B. Plevan (Council on Judicial Administration), Alice Henkin (International Human Rights), and Carol Bellamy (Legal Problems of the Mentally Ill).[11] During Kaufman's presidency, more than sixty committees undertook a review of women's issues in their areas. By 1987, the fiftieth anniversary of the election of the first woman member of the Association, there were seven women among the twenty-two members of the Executive Committee and two on the seven-person Nominating Committee. The first woman chair of the Executive Committee, Joan L. Ellenbogen, served during the 1987–88 year. Since then, there have been three more: Barbara Paul Robinson, Barbara Dale Underwood, and Beatrice S. Frank. In May 1989, a Special Committee on Women in the Profession was formed, chaired by Bettina B. Plevan, a partner at Proskauer Rose Goetz & Mendelsohn. One-third of the committee chairs appointed in 1990 were women. By 1992, there were forty-two female committee chairs.[12]

One of the most compelling committee documents of the past twenty-five years is that on "Sexual Harassment in the Lawyers' Workplace," published in the November 1991 *Record* and essentially a transcript of a panel discussion that had taken place in the House.[13] Under EEOC guidelines sexual harassment can be either harassment as a *quid pro quo* for receiving employment benefits or the creation of a hostile work environment. Some months before the panel discussion occurred, a survey of women associates and partners throughout the country was published in the *National Law Journal*. Sixty percent reported having experienced some form of harassment in the legal workplace, encompassing sexual teasing, cornering and pinching, pressure for sex, and even rape. Alexander Forger, chairman of Milbank Tweed at the time, reported that, even after years of publishing and republishing the firm's policy on sexual harassment, almost half the employees responded that they were unfamiliar with the policy, more than half did not know where to report any incident of sexual harassment, and more than fifty percent responded that they would not feel comfortable reporting such an incident.[14] In 1993 the Committee on Labor and Employment Law offered a model policy for dealing with sexual harassment which included a warning that, even in consenting romantic and sexual relationships, each person "should be aware of the possible risks." On the other hand, the sexual harassment policy was not intended to "be used as a basis for excluding or separating individuals of a particular gender from participating in business or work-related social activities or discussions."[15]

Among the recent committee reports dealing with gender equality are those of the Committee on Military Affairs and Justice on "Equality for Women in Combat Aviation," which concluded that the refusal to let women compete for these positions probably violates the Equal Protection guarantees of the Fifth Amendment,[16] and of the Committee on Women in the Profession on the need for and viability of flexible work arrangements in the New York legal community.[17]

In 1992 the Special Committee on Women in the Profession commissioned a study of the conditions that inhibit the advancement of women in the legal profession. Written by Cynthia Fuchs Epstein, the study, "Glass Ceilings and Open Doors: Women's Advancement in the Legal Profession," was published in the November 1995 *Fordham Law Review*, just after commemoration of the 125th anniversary.[18]

THE ASSOCIATION AND ISSUES OF SEXUAL PREFERENCE

In the past twenty-five years, the basic stance of the Association toward virtually all (law-abiding) groups has been for inclusion. That includes gay men and lesbians. In 1973 the American Psychiatric Association voted to remove "homosexuality" from its list of mental defects, disorders, and sexual deviations. Shortly thereafter, municipalities began adapting anti-discrimination legislation to apply to sexual preference. During the 1970s the Association supported laws prohibiting discrimination on the basis of sexual preference at the local, state, and federal levels and also supported repeal of the laws against sodomy. In January 1973, the Special Committee on Sex and Law, chaired by Merrell E. Clark, Jr., and the Committee on Civil Rights, chaired by Maria L. Marcus, urged adoption of municipal legislation to prohibit discrimination in employment, places of accommodation, and in housing accommodations based on a person's sexual orientation.[19] Several months later, the Special Committee on Sex and Law and the Committee on Criminal Courts, Law and Procedure chaired by Michael Juviler urged repeal of the state statute making consensual sodomy a crime.[20] In both cases, however, the actual titles given the reports gave no hint to a casual reader as to what the subject matter might be.

In 1976 the Special Committee on Sex and Law chaired by Carol Bellamy urged passage by Congress of a law that would have prohibited discrimination on the bases of affectional or sexual preference in public accommodations, public education, employment, housing, and rental accommodations.[21]

In the 1980s, the Association took the position that anti-sodomy laws were unconstitutional, urged removal of homosexuality as a ground to exclude aliens from admission to the United States, and directed attention to the problem of AIDS in prisons. The Committee on Sex and Law unsuccessfully argued in an *amicus* brief in the Supreme Court in the case of *Bowers v. Hardwick*[22] that the Georgia sodomy statute should be held unconstitutional.[23] In a report published in 1985, the Committee on Immigration and Nationality Law, noting that the United States, "alone among all the nations of the world, statutorily excludes homosexual persons from admission into the country for any purpose whatsoever," urged removing homosexuality as a ground for exclusion from the United States. Indeed, the *de facto* policy of the Immigration and Naturalization Service in 1985 was essentially to look the other way unless the homosexuality was brought to its attention. The United States, the committee said, "should no longer permit a mere historical stigma to serve as the basis for exclusion of persons with no other excludable defect."[24]

The Association has not been mute in AIDS matters. As has already been seen, the Joint Subcommittee on AIDS in the Criminal Justice System rendered reports in 1987 and 1989 on the handling of AIDS by the criminal justice systems of state and city (p. 130).

In 1989, the Committees on Legal Issues Affecting People with Disabilities, Medicine and Law, Sex and Law, and AIDS filed briefs in two cases, which argued that the offices of an orthopedic surgeon and a dentist were "places of public accommodation" and, therefore, covered by the Human Rights Law, so that medical professionals could not refuse patients with AIDS.[25]

In 1990 the Association created the Committee on Lesbians and Gay Men in the Profession, the second such bar association committee in the nation. That committee has been very active. In 1991, the Committee, co-chaired by Judge Joan Lobis and Arthur Leonard, urged Governor Mario Cuomo to uphold the finding of the State Division of Human Rights that SUNY Buffalo violated his Executive Order by permitting on-campus recruiting by the Judge Advocate General Corps of the U.S. military, because the military discriminates on the basis of sexual orientation.[26] The policy of non-discrimination adopted by the Executive Committee for the Association in 1992 (p. 141) was initially prepared by the Committee on Lesbians and Gay Men in the Profession.[27]

However, other committees have also been active in this area in recent years. In 1991–92, the Ad Hoc Committee on AIDS fought the reduction of funding for AIDS research, testified on HIV guidelines before the Federal Centers for Disease Control, commented on AIDS testing by private laboratories and criticized a rule regarding AIDS examinations of aliens, while the McKay Community Outreach Law Program trained lawyers to represent women suffering from AIDS.[28] In 1992 the Committee on Sex and Law concluded that granting second-parent adoption in New York State in the context of gay and lesbian families not only was permissible under the Domestic Relations Law, but served as well to further the traditional family law goal of advancing children's best interests.[29]

Two important reports were published in 1993. The Committee on

Federal Legislation urged the rejection of the "don't ask, don't tell" approach of the Clinton Administration to the issue of homosexuality in the armed forces, arguing forcefully that the compromise was unwise and unconstitutional, whether strict scrutiny applied or even a test of mere rationality.[30] The Committee on Lesbians and Gay Men in the Profession wrote of the slightly more subtle form of discriminatory treatment affecting the culture of the workplace for gay and lesbian attorneys:

> Lesbian and gay attorneys who are placed in the uncomfortable position of having to hide their sexual orientation, and, in many cases, their lives outside the strict confines of the workplace, are denied participation in an important component of the daily informal networking within legal organizations, part of the social interaction between colleagues that normally leads to a more productive workplace and to greater opportunities for individual advancement. The pressures to hide a part of their identity, and the energy expended in doing so, also imposes on lesbians and gay men a great burden, not similarly borne by their heterosexual colleagues, that may affect an employee's performance.[31]

THE ASSOCIATION AND THE HOMELESS

John Feerick and Barbara Paul Robinson have strongly supported the Association's outreach efforts. Robinson, for example, has emphasized that: "We, as a bar association, are totally committed to community outreach, at both the policy and [the] advocacy levels, as well as to providing direct services to the disadvantaged through our volunteers."[32]

The Association's work with the homeless, which began under Oliensis, may be taken as emblematic of the outreach efforts. After reviewing the problem of homelessness for two years, the Committee on Legal Problems of the Homeless, chaired by Robert P. Patterson, Jr., delivered a sixty-two–page report on November 1, 1988. The committee wrote of the "human tragedies"—of what it saw, but could not completely feel:

... the homeless whose plight is unseen, ignored, or forgotten. We do not feel the stigma and pain suffered by children branded "hotel kids" by their schoolmates. We cannot feel hunger in the stomachs of children who are fed on a "restaurant allowance" of $1.10 per meal. Most dare not look inside a shelter for homeless adults. There, the disabled agonize their way up flights of stairs; diabetics store insulin on window sills for want of refrigeration; disabilities are aggravated rather than eliminated; human beings are warehoused rather than treated.[33]

The committee pointed out that "homelessness has, in large measure, been precipitated by action or inaction on the part of our government—federal, state or local."[34] It was caused by the freezing of maximum shelter allowances, the abandonment by the city of *in rem* buildings, the end of the state residential housing construction program, the release of mental patients without support services, and the Reagan Administration cutback in entitlements.

The committee called for many changes. There were a series of specific recommendations, one of the most important of which was a reasonable public assistance allowance for shelter. The Project on the Homeless was created to follow up on the "Patterson Report." Harold R. Tyler, Jr., was chair; Allan L. Gropper, vice-chair. In the meantime, the Committee on Legal Assistance had studied pilot programs, including its Housing Court project (p. 137), and concluded that legal assistance made an impressive difference in presenting evidence and, ultimately, in reducing homelessness.[35] The committee strongly recommended expansion of state-funded programs providing legal representation to poor persons threatened with eviction at the earliest stage of the process.

On November 1, 1989, the Project on the Homeless filed a motion for leave to appear as *amicus curiae* in the Court of Appeals in the case of *Jiggetts v. Grinker*. The Project argued that the Patterson Committee had analyzed the same provisions of the law, legislative history, and relevant regulations as the First Department had in its *Jiggetts* decision "and yet arrived at a far different construction of the Social Services Law." The project argued that the Appellate Division's decision would eviscerate the statutory language requiring the New York State Department of Social Services to provide adequate shelter allowances to keep dependent children in their homes. The Appellate Division had, the Project argued, reached its result by "reliance on a cross-reference contained in a law that says the exact opposite." The Project urged the Court of Appeals not to "leave standing the legerdemain of the Appellate Division."[36]

The Project was successful in the Court of Appeals. Although further litigation in the case has dragged on for four years, a *modus vivendi* was worked out between Legal Aid and New York State, so that any tenant can get an emergency grant or "*Jiggetts* intervention."[37]

In a June 1992 report on the Mayor's Implementation Plan, originally distributed as a letter to the Mayor and to the Speaker of the New York City Council, the Project prodded the mayor, city council, and state to do more, more rapidly.[38]

On June 19, 1991, the Association launched a weekly clinic to provide free on-site legal counseling to the homeless population. Every Wednesday from 6 p.m. to 9 p.m. at the St. Agnes Drop-In Center at 152 East 44th Street, which serves the Grand Central area, eight to twelve volunteers—lawyers, law students, and paralegals (backed up by twenty-five mentors)—assisted forty to sixty people. In addition, one clinic was held at a different shelter once each month. From May 1, 1992 to August 13, 1992, 1,897 cases were assigned to volunteers. Of this, 1,447 cases involved counseling, and 450 involved direct representation. Lawyers from large firms to solo practitioners and law students have participated. While the major need addressed at these clinics is information about entitlement programs, many have been advised on adoptions, foster care, abuse and neglect proceedings, and lost or stolen alien registration cards. Referrals to drug- and alcohol-treatment programs and free medical clinics are also made.[39]

In 1994, Hunton & Williams' New York office formed a *pro bono* partnership with the Association by "adopting" the St. Agnes Drop-In Center. Hunton & Williams personnel are trained by a Community Outreach staff attorney and are supervised by Outreach staff.[40] The Legal Clinic for the Homeless has since expanded to include several additional sites.

Writing about his own experience visiting the clinic and sitting with half-a-dozen other volunteer lawyers, Conrad Harper mused,

"Seeing the homeless reminds us how vulnerable each of us is. No one has absolute power against deprivation. In the long arc of life it is certain that we shall be touched as well by tragedy as by good fortune. We should help while we can before our own needs exceed our capacity to help others."[41]

To give but one example of the work of the homeless clinic: A victim of domestic violence lost her apartment when she left the marital home for a city shelter and was forced to place her three young children in foster care. After she sought assistance at the clinic, her lawyer informed her that the city's Human Resources Administration provides grants to reunite parents with their children if their children have been in foster care for at least thirty days and the parent lacks adequate housing. The client was able to obtain this grant and was subsequently able to rent an apartment and be reunited with her children.[42]

COMMITTEES

By the end of John Feerick's presidency, the Association had 184 committees.[43] Newly established committees of the Feerick tenure included the Advisory Committee on Alternative Dispute Resolution, the Task Force on International Legal Services, the Committee on the Thurgood Marshall Summer Law Internship Program, and the Ad Hoc Committee on the Association's 125th Anniversary.

As so often has been the case over the past twenty-five years, the Committee on Federal Legislation between 1992 and 1995 rendered a number of reports of general interest. Returning to the weaknesses of the electoral college twenty-four years after the Association had issued its last report on the subject,[44] the committee again called for direct election of the President.[45] The committee reported on the constitutionality of gun control legislation, concluding that the Second Amendment "presents no bar whatsoever" to proposed gun control legislation.[46] In the April 1995 *Record*, there were reports from the Federal Legislation Committee on three major subjects: the application of federal laws to Congress, the proposed balanced budget amendment to the Constitution, and the line-item veto. Reviewing a bill different in some respects from the one that became the Congressional Accountability Act of January 23, 1995,[47] the committee was troubled by the problem of Congress's desiring to grant its employees the substantive protection of the laws without subjecting itself to enforcement by the executive branch.[48] On the balanced budget amendment, the committee concluded that a balanced budget is not an appropriate subject for a constitutional amendment and that, if an amendment were ever adopted, it would lead to at least two troubling consequences—judicial oversight of budgetary decisions and control of fiscal policy by a legislative minority.[49] The Committee concluded that line-item veto legislation is unconstitutional, because it violates the Veto Clause of the Constitution and the constitutionally mandated separation of powers.[50]

The May 1995 *Record* contained an evaluation by the Committee on Federal Legislation of two proposed changes to the exclusionary rule—an extension of the good faith exception to include situations where the officer had an "objectively reasonable belief" that his/her conduct is in conformity with the Constitution, and an abrogation of the rule entirely and its replacement by a tort remedy. The committee recommended against passage of either proposal.[51]

Nevertheless, the Committee on Federal Legislation did not have a monopoly on subjects of broad general interest. One of the most important reports in recent years was the joint report of the Committee on International Arms Control and Security Affairs and the Committee on International Law on the U.S. Military Action in Panama.[52] The committees chose to study the rationales put forward by the Bush Administration for the overthrow of the Noriega regime—rationales which, once the invasion was over, were not explored by either the Congress or the media. The committees reported "two keen surprises":

> The problem of violence faced by American armed service personnel and civilians in Panama was longstanding and more serious than generally reported in the press. But equally surprising is the United States' extended failure to implement other available methods for thwarting the police brutality faced by Americans in Panama. This passivity undermines the claim of self-defense as a ground for invasion.

The use of force in international affairs is governed by the requirements of necessity and proportionality; the United States' action re-
mains vulnerable under these standards.[53]

In 1993, the Committee on Administrative Law reviewed current
dispute resolution procedures at New York City's welfare centers and
made recommendations for improving the procedures, which could
both benefit welfare recipients and reduce costs.[54] In April 1995,
seven committees—Children and the Law, Civil Rights, Immigration
and Nationality Law, Family Court and Family Law, Legal Assistance, Legal Issues Affecting People with Disabilities, and Legal
Needs of the Poor—and the Project on the Homeless reviewed legislation pending in Congress that would eliminate many federally
funded programs, replacing them with block grants to the states. The
committees called the legislation "irrational" and "dangerous" and
could "see no possible justification for an approach that would
achieve increased levels of hunger, malnutrition, disease and family
dysfunction among our nation's most vulnerable, at considerable
public expense." The committees said that the legislation would "ensure misery and hardship, without any significant likelihood of
achieving a short- or long-term benefit."[55]

THE 125TH ANNIVERSARY

The 125th anniversary of the Association is being commemorated by
a series of symposia; a campaign to raise money to build an extension
to the House, which will hold a state-of-the-art training center for
the McKay COLP, and to seed an endowment for its outreach activities; a gala celebration at Lincoln Center; and the publication of this
history. The Ad Hoc Committee on the Association's 125th Anniversary was chaired by Barry H. Garfinkel. Among its fourteen members
were nine men and women who had served as presidents of the Association. The first symposium, held on December 1, 1994, was devoted to the future of elementary and secondary education and
included a series of workshops on such topics as school restructuring
and governance and gender equity. The second symposium in the

series, held on February 9, 1995, dealt with economic development, jobs, and welfare in New York City, The keynote speaker was Richard A. Kahan, president of the Urban Assembly. The third symposium, held on April 25th, dealt with public safety, crime, and civil rights. Among those who participated were Philip Heymann of the Harvard Law faculty; Raymond Kelly, former New York City Police Commissioner; and Burt Neuborne of New York University School of Law. The fourth symposium was held on June 15th and was devoted to the subject of health care access. The keynote speaker was Donna Shalala, Secretary of Health and Human Services. The fifth, held on November 15, 1995, was on lawyers in the public service. During the 125th anniversary year, Mary Robinson, president of Ireland, and Judith S. Kaye, Chief Judge of the New York Court of Appeals, were named the fifty-first and fifty-second Honorary Members of the Association.

On Wednesday evening September 13, the Association celebrated its 125th anniversary at a gala reception at Avery Fisher Hall, Lincoln Center. Five of the seven speakers were women attorneys and judges.* Barbara Paul Robinson emphasized the vibrancy, energy, and effectiveness of the Association.[56] Mayor Rudolph Giuliani spoke of New York City as "the capital of the world for the practice of law" and stated that the City owed "its national and international preeminence in the legal profession to the very high standards of professional excellence that is set in New York City and that are maintained, and the Association of the Bar is critical to both the setting and maintaining of these standards."[57]

Speaking by videotape (because she had attended the Beijing Conference on Women), Hillary Rodham Clinton spoke of the Association's Community Outreach Law Program, while Chief Judge Judith S. Kaye narrated a video on the program work of the McKay COLP.[58] American Bar Association President, Roberta Cooper Ramo, spoke of the founding fathers of the City Bar as having "set a paradigm: the idea, the key of a bar association would be its commitment to public service."[59]

---

*On October 18, 1995, the Association honored at a Municipal Breakfast Forum another distinguished female practitioner, Edith Spivack, who had completed sixty-one years of public service at the New York City Law Department.

Finally, Justice Ruth Bader Ginsburg noted that women accounted for 25 percent of the Association's membership and 35 per cent of the committee chairs and that the Association was "all the richer for the diversity of its members' talent and experience."[60] She concluded with the aspiration: "May the Association of the Bar of the City of New York thrive in housing . . . people concerned about the society law exists to serve, people who will, as the prophet Micah said, 'do justice and love mercy.'"[61]

A few days after the commemoration, *The New York Times* editorialized that the Association had celebrated its 125th anniversary in a public-minded fashion, "honoring its duty to help provide fair access to the justice system."[62] Indeed, the 125th anniversary capital campaign, chaired by Cyrus R. Vance, had surpassed its $3 million goal. The funds will be used to construct space in the House for a new home for the Community Outreach Law Program, now scattered in the Bar Building, with offices and a training facility. That, in turn, is part of the construction of six stories in the building courtyard to consolidate the entire Association staff in the House.[63]

*   *   *

Had the men who came together in the winter of 1870 to form The Association of the Bar of the City of New York been able to attend the 125th anniversary commemoration, they would no doubt have been surprised at how the organization has flourished in a more democratic and egalitarian age. It is unlikely that they would have celebrated with enthusiasm the heterogeneity of the Association's membership and they would undoubtedly have been dumbfounded at some of the newer functions of the organization. Nevertheless, one suspects that the Founders would have recognized and respected the manner in which the expertise of the membership and reputation of the Association have been put behind its public-spirited activities.

True to its Founders, the Association, during the past twenty-five years, has spoken out with effect on great matters of concern not only to attorneys—most notably on Vietnam, Carswell, and Bork. True to its Founders, but with more effect, the Association has addressed those areas of state and municipal judicial selection and judicial administration that have concerned it since its earliest days. Nor has the Association forgotten about the municipality in which it is based, coming to its assistance during a time of very great challenge. More sensitive than its founders to the role of its Great City as the home of the "tired, [the] poor, [the] . . . huddled masses yearning to breathe free," the City Bar has pursued a policy of inclusion and tolerance both within and outside the Association during a period in which its nation has been neither "kinder" nor "gentler." This, in turn, has led to the use of its unrivaled resource, its membership, to serve as attorneys for those unable to hire one. In doing so, the Association of the Bar has been yet again the pacesetter for the nation's bar associations. In this, it has added yet another side to Louis Dembitz Brandeis's recognition that lawyering offers " 'an opportunity for usefulness which is probably unrivalled' "[64]—acting, as Barbara Paul Robinson put it, "to renew our sense of community."[65]

NOTES

1. *From Failing Hands: The Story of Presidential Succession* (New York: Fordham University Press, 1965). A decade later, Feerick wrote *The Twenty-Fifth Amendment: Its Complete History and Applications* (New York: Fordham University Press, 1976; 2nd ed. 1992).

2. *Milwaukee Journal*, May 18, 1995.

3. Interview with John D. Feerick (see above, chap. 1, note 2).

4. Conrad K. Harper, "Remarks: Presentation of the Harper Portrait to the Association, Nov. 16, 1993," *The Record*, 49 (January/February 1994), 19. Interviews with Conrad Harper (see above, chap. 3, note 1) and John D. Feerick (see above, chap. 1, note 2).

5. "Interview with Barbara Paul Robinson, President of the Association of the Bar of the City of New York," *Metropolitan Corporate Counsel* (August 1994); *New York Times*, November 19, 1993, p. A30.

6. Barbara Paul Robinson, "Inaugural Address," *The Record*, 49 (December 1994), 927.

7. Barbara Paul Robinson, "President's Column: Children Are Our Future," *44th Street Notes*, 10, No. 5 (May 1995) 2.

8. *The Record*, 49 (December 1994), 931.

9. See Abel, *American Lawyers* (see above, chap. 3, note 33), pp. 90ff., esp. p. 98. Generally, see Anthony P. Grech and Daniel J. Jacobs, "Women and the Legal Profession: A Bibliography of Current Literature," *The Record*, 44 (March 1989), 215–29.

10. Powell, *From Patrician to Professional Elite* (see above, chap. 1, note 2), p. 64.

11. *The Record*, 41 (October 1986), 680–83.

12. See *The Record*, 43 (January/February 1988), 2, 3; Robert M. Kaufman, "Farewell Address," *The Record*, 43 (November 1988), 775.

13. Committee on Women in the Profession, "Sexual Harassment in the Lawyers' Workplace," *The Record*, 46 (November 1991), 728.

14. Ibid., 745.

15. Committee on Labor and Employment Law, "Law Firm Policies on Workplace Sexual Harassment," *The Record*, 48 (March 1993), 179, 185, 186, 190.

16. *The Record*, 48 (April 1993), 326.

17. Committee on Women in the Profession, "A Report on the Need for, Availability and Viability of Flexible Work Arrangements in the New York Legal Community," *The Record*, 50 (June 1995), 522.

18. Barbara Paul Robinson, "President's Column: Promoting Diversity in the Profession," *44th Street Notes*, 11, No. 1 (January 1996), 1. See also *44th Street Notes*, 7, No. 9 (November 1992) 1, 3.

19. "New York City Council Intro. No. 475," *The Record*, 28 (February 1973), 148 (Feb. 1973). See also *New York Times*, November 9, 1978.

20. "New York S.3472 and S.4107; A.3404 and A.3545," *The Record*, 28 (May 1973), 380.

21. "Federal Legislation Prohibiting Discrimination on the Basis of Affectional or Sexual Preference," *The Record*, 31 (May/June 1976), 363.

22. 478 U.S. 186 (1986).

23. *The Record*, 41 (April 1986), 302.

24. Ibid., 47.

25. See *The Record*, 44 (November 1989), 646; *The Record*, 44 (December 1989), 805. The cases were *Elstein v. N.Y.S. Div. of Human Rights* and *Hurwitz v. New York City Commission on Human Rights*.

26. *The Record*, 47 (November 1991), 718.

27. *The Record*, 47 (May 1992), 352. See also Harper, "Farewell Address" (see above, chap. 6, note 25), 585.

28. Conrad K. Harper, "President's Column: AIDS, Magic and Struggle," *44th Street Notes*, 7, No. 2 (February 1992), 1–2.

29. Committee on Sex and Law, "Second Parent Adoption in New York State: Furthering the Best Interests of Our Children," *The Record*, 47 (December 1992), 983.

30. Committee on Federal Legislation, "The Ban on Military Service by Lesbians and Gay Men," *The Record*, 48 (June 1993), 645.

31. Committee on Lesbians and Gay Men in the Profession, "Report on the Experience of Lesbians and Gay Men in the Legal Profession," *The Record*, 48 (November 1993), 843.

32. Interview with Barbara Paul Robinson (see above, note 5).

33. "Report of the Committee on the Legal Problems of the Homeless," *The Record*, 44 (January/February 1988), 35.

34. Ibid., 33.

35. Committee on Legal Assistance, "Preventing Homelessness through Representation of Tenants Faced with Eviction," *The Record*, 44 (April 1989), 234.

36. Affidavit of Allan L. Gropper in Support of the Motion of the Project on the Homeless of the Association of the Bar of the City of New York to Appear as *Amicus Curiae* and for Leave to File Memorandum as amicus Curiae in Support of the

Motion for Leave to Appeal, *Jiggetts v. Grinker* (Index No. 40582/87; Sup. Ct., N.Y. Co.) (November 1, 1989).

37. Interview with Allan L. Gropper, February 23, 1995.

38. Project on the Homeless, "New York City's Policies on the Homeless," *The Record*, 47 (November 1992), 872.

39. "Legal Clinics for the Homeless a Success," *44th Street Notes*, 7, No. 2 (February 1992), 6.

40. *The Record*, 49 (April 1994), 275.

41. "President's Column: Homelessness," *44th Street Notes*, 7, No. 3 (March 1992), 2.

42. William J. Dean, "Legal Clinics for the Homeless," *New York Law Journal*, September 27, 1993.

43. John D. Feerick, "Farewell Address" (see above, chap. 7, note 20), 920.

44. Committee on Federal Legislation, "Proposed Constitutional Amendment Providing for Direct Election of President and Vice President," *The Record*, 24 (May 1969), 285.

45. Committee on Federal Legislation, "Proposed Constitutional Amendment Providing for Direct Election of the President and the Vice-President of the United States," *The Record*, 48 (November 1993), 821.

46. "Federal Gun Control and the Second Amendment," *The Record*, 48 (December 1993), 993.

47. P.L. 104–1.

48. "The Applicability of Federal Laws to Congress," *The Record*, 50 (April 1995), 270.

49. "Amending the Constitution to Require a Balanced Budget," *The Record*, 50 (April 1995), 305.

50. "Revisiting the Line-Item Veto," *The Record*, 50 (April 1995), 321. The earlier report of the Committee on Federal Legislation was "The Line-Item Veto," *The Record*, 41 (1986), 367.

51. Committee on Federal Legislation, "Proposed Changes to the Exclusionary Rule," *The Record*, 50 (May 1995), 385.

52. "The Use of Armed Force in International Affairs: The Case of Panama," *The Record*, 47 (October, 1992), 604.

53. Ibid., 608–609.

54. Committee on Administrative Law, "Dispute Resolution in the Welfare System: Toward an End to the Fair Hearing Overload," *The Record*, 48 (May 1993), 411.

55. "Report and Recommendations on H.R.4, 'The Personal Responsibility Act of 1995,'" *The Record*, 50 (June 1995), 493, 516, 517.

56. Barbara Paul Robinson, "Welcome and Remarks in The Association of the Bar of the City of New York's 125th Anniversary Gala at Lincoln Center," *The Record*, 50, No. 8 (December 1995), 830.

57. Ibid., 832, 833.

58. Ibid., 830, 835.

59. Ibid., 836, 837.

60. Ibid., 839, 840.

61. Ibid.

62. *New York Times*, October 18, 1995.

63. Barbara Paul Robinson, "President's Column: 125 Years—A Gala Celebration," *44th Street Notes*, 10, No. 8 (September 1995), 1, 2.

64. The phrase is from Brandeis' *The Opportunity in the Law*, quoted in Geoffrey C. Hazard, Jr., and Deborah L. R. Rohde, *The Legal Profession's Responsibility and Regulation* (Westbury, N.Y.: Foundation Press, 1988), p. 20.

65. Barbara Paul Robinson, "Inaugural Address" (see above, note 6), 931.

Index

International Human Rights, Committee on, 61, 87–90, 161
International Law, Committee on, 169
International Legal Services, Task Force on, 168
International Trade, Committee on, 128
Iovenko, Michael, 160

Jackson, Robert, 13
Javits, Jacob K., 1, 32, 33, 117
Jensen, Grady E., 99
Jessup, Philip C., 30
Johnson, Lyndon B., 8, 46, 47
Johnston, Neal, 36
Judd, Orren, 60
Judicial Administration. Council on, 161
Judicial selection, 45, 53–57, 81, 104–105, 125–126, 172
Judiciary, Committee on the, 12, 97, 105, 120, 134, 135
Juviler, Michael, 163

Karpatkin, Rhoda H., 80
Kasanof, Robert, 80
Kass, Stephen C., 38, 89
Kaufman, Irving R., 58, 62, 126
Kaufman, Robert M., 6, 38, 60, 80, 96, 97, 98, 111, 116–118, 119, 120, 121, 122–123, 128, 148, 161
Kaye, Judith S., 56, 97, 110, 171
Kennedy, Anthony, 121, 122; nomination to Supreme Court, 122, 123, 124
Kennedy, John F., 6, 46
King, Martin Luther, Jr., 5–6, 47
Kleindienst, Richard, 48
Klots, Allen, 71
Knapp, Whitman, 33
Knapp [Whitman] Commission (Commission to Investigate Police Corruption in New York City), 47
Koch, Edward I., 82–83, 111, 128, 148
Kovner, Victor, 55, 148
Kramer, George P., 36

Kunstler, William, 52
Kurtz, Daniel L., 108

Labor and Employment Law, Committee on, 112, 129, 162
Labor and Social Security Legislation, Committee on, 7, 87
Lang, Jonathan, 152
Largi, Linda, 99
The Law of Impeachment, 50
Law Student Perspectives, Committee on, 158
Lawyer advertising, 45, 58, 67, 78–80
Lawyer Advertising, Committee on, 134
Lawyers' Committee for Civil Rights Under Law, 6, 134, 135
Lawyers Committee for Effective Action to End the Vietnam War, 26
Lawyers Convocation on Vietnam, 26, 27
Lawyers in Transition Program, 145, 158; Lawyers in Transition, Committee on, 145
Lawyers' Placement Bureau, Committee on, 22
Lawyer's Role in the Search for Peace, Committee on, 68
Lawyer's Role in Tax Practice, Committee on, 112
The Legal Aid Society, 39, 52, 53, 73, 81, 98, 106, 116, 117, 134, 146, 167
Legal Assistance, Committee on, 106, 109, 112, 137, 166, 170
Legal Clinic for the Homeless, 167
Legal Education and Admission to the Bar, Committee on, 135
Legal Issues Affecting People with Disabilities, Committee on, 164, 170
Legal Needs of the Poor, Committee on, 170
Legal Problems of the Aging, Committee on, 128, 139, 152
Legal Problems of the Homeless, Committee on, 165–166